T0300900

un journaling

Some students are just not comfortable with sharing intimate details about their thoughts, feelings, and lives—at least, not with others in a class or group. *Unjournaling, Second Edition* is brimming with playful writing prompts that are entirely impersonal, easing the way for hesitant writers while still offering creative challenges for those who are more experienced.

This edition updates existing prompts while introducing 50 brand new ones. It includes sample responses—a helpful tool for anyone who gets stuck with a topic and wants to see how it can be done! Two examples of the 250 writing prompts include:

- Somebody's sitting behind you on the bus. You hear only one side of an odd cell phone conversation, but it is intriguing and alarms you. What do you hear?
- Igor could hardly wait to get his new special license plates for his car. He paid extra for these plates: BIM-BB1. Explain the meaning behind this very special license plate.

Suited for seventh grade to adulthood, *Unjournaling* is a flexible, varied, interesting, and, most of all, *fun* approach to creative writing.

un journaling

**Daily writing exercises that are
NOT personal
NOT introspective
NOT boring!**

SECOND EDITION

Dawn DiPrince & Cheryl Miller Thurston

Routledge
Taylor & Francis Group

NEW YORK AND LONDON

Cover illustration: Larry Nolte

Second edition published 2023
by Routledge
605 Third Avenue, New York, NY 10158

and by Routledge
4 Park Square, Milton Park, Abingdon, Oxon, OX14 4RN

Routledge is an imprint of the Taylor & Francis Group, an informa business

© 2023 Dawn DiPrince and Cheryl Miller Thurston

The right of Dawn DiPrince and Cheryl Miller Thurston to be identified as authors of this work has been asserted in accordance with sections 77 and 78 of the Copyright, Designs and Patents Act 1988.

All rights reserved. The purchase of this copyright material confers the right on the purchasing institution to photocopy pages which bear the copyright line at the bottom of the page. No other parts of this book may be reprinted or reproduced or utilised in any form or by any electronic, mechanical, or other means, now known or hereafter invented, including photocopying and recording, or in any information storage or retrieval system, without permission in writing from the publishers.

Trademark notice: Product or corporate names may be trademarks or registered trademarks and are used only for identification and explanation without intent to infringe.

First edition published by Prufrock Press Inc. 2006

Library of Congress Cataloging-in-Publication Data
Names: DiPrince, Dawn, author. | Thurston, Cheryl Miller, 1949– author.
Title: Unjournaling : daily writing exercises that are not personal,
not introspective, not boring! / Dawn DiPrince & Cheryl Miller Thurston.
Description: Second edition. | New York, NY : Routledge, 2023. |
Summary: Provided by publisher.
Identifiers: LCCN 2022031040 (print) | LCCN 2022031041 (ebook) |
ISBN 9781032244280 (hardback) | ISBN 9781032227467 (paperback) |
ISBN 9781003278559 (ebook)
Subjects: LCSH: English language–Composition and exercises. | Creative writing.
Classification: LCC LB1631 .D548 2023 (print) |
LCC LB1631 (ebook) | DDC 808/.042–dc23/eng/20220707
LC record available at https://lccn.loc.gov/2022031040
LC ebook record available at https://lccn.loc.gov/2022031041

ISBN: 978-1-032-24428-0 (hbk)
ISBN: 978-1-032-22746-7 (pbk)
ISBN: 978-1-003-27855-9 (ebk)

DOI: 10.4324/9781003278559

Typeset in Goudy
by Newgen Publishing UK

Contents

Introduction

Writing can be an intimidating process for many people, no matter what their age. It can be revealing—too revealing. Some people just don't want to share intimate details about their thoughts, feelings and lives, at least not with others in a class or group. They may not have the level of trust necessary, and quite possibly for very good reason. Or they may not have the confidence necessary. Or they may simply be very private people.

Writing does not have to be a psychological journey, and neither does it have to be limited to reports and other fact-based work. All the playful daily writing prompts in *Unjournaling* are entirely impersonal, easing the way for hesitant writers while still challenging the creativity of more experienced writers. They take writers out of themselves and involve them in playing with words, inventing characters, imagining and writing about situations involving others, and much more.

Most of all, *Unjournaling* encourages students of all ages to have fun with language. Some of the writing prompts may seem silly, but we have learned that silly writing can really help writers loosen up.

In an educational world hemmed in by high-stakes testing, there is a very specific purpose for low-stakes creative writing. Both emerging and experienced writers benefit from playing with language, taking risks, and experimenting with words. The activities in *Unjournaling* build writing muscle in the same way that regular running gives a person the muscles to run a 5k. They also help writers build trust in themselves, their abilities, and—most importantly—their own voices.

Studies have shown that writing instruction that centers on rules and formulas has the opposite effect. Such an approach can even make students worse writers by eroding confidence in their use of language. Rules are important, but they exist to enable communication—not to hinder it by

DOI: 10.4324/9781003278559-1

creating writers and speakers so concerned with following the rules that they second guess what they are saying.

This new edition of *Unjournaling* includes 50 new prompts as well as updates to the earlier edition of the book. Teachers can use *Unjournaling* in the classroom, or individuals can use it on their own. Writing classes for adults have also used the prompts as warm-ups and challenges.

Sample responses to all of the questions are included in the last part of the book—a helpful resource for teachers or anyone who gets stuck completing a prompt and wants to see that it *can* be done. Reading what others have written can also open a writer's mind to different approaches that he or she may not have considered.

We have tried to make the writing prompts in this book flexible, varied, challenging, interesting, and even fun to do. We hope you enjoy *Unjournaling!*

Dawn DiPrince and Cheryl Miller Thurston

un journaling

Writing Prompts

DOI: 10.4324/9781003278559-2

1. Write a paragraph about a girl named Dot, but use no letters with dots (i, j).

2. *Silly* is wearing flip-flops to school in a blizzard.

Silly is a golden retriever who slinks sheepishly off the sofa whenever his owner comes home, hoping—despite the piles of hair all over the cushion—that she won't notice he's been sleeping there.

Silly is a chocolate frosting-faced five-year-old who denies sneaking a chocolate cupcake.

What else is *silly*? Give three more examples.

3. Write a paragraph that includes at least ten words that rhyme with *be*.

4. Write a paragraph about a cat attacking something, but don't use the words *hiss*, *scratch*, or *pounce*.

5. Describe the gunky stuff that gets caught in the basket at the bottom of the sink. Don't use the words *disgusting* or *gross*.

6. A bad dude in a cowboy hat is walking into the saloon in a bad Western movie. He's looking dangerous and mad. Tell what happens, creating a happy ending.

7.
Write a paragraph that includes 20 words with double vowels. Examples: *poodle*, *peep*, *needle*.

8. How many ways can you find to say no? Write ten sentences that say no in various ways, but without using the word no.

9. When you write, it is important to fit your tone to your purpose. If you want the manager of Widget World to allow a return, even though the 30-day return period has passed, it's not a good idea to start your email to the manager in this hostile tone: "I don't know what knucklehead came up with your policy, but I think it's stupid."

If you want to apply for a job at Widget World, it's not a good idea to send a text to the manager in this casual tone: "Hey. I hear you need a Widget wonk, and I'm cool with that."

If you want to propose marriage to the manager of Widget World, it's probably not a good idea to start your letter in this formal tone: "Dear Ms. Applespot: After a careful analysis, I find that a legal partnership, i.e. marriage, between the two of us would be beneficial to both parties involved."

To match tone to purpose, use words that fit the circumstances. Imagine you are an employee at of Widget World. You have been hoping for a raise, since you know you've done an excellent job. However, the owner of the store isn't exactly the sharpest knife in the drawer, in your opinion, and probably hasn't even noticed. Write a letter to the owner, choosing your tone carefully as you point out why you should have that raise.

10. Create a sentence with words that begin with the letters in *sentence*, in order. In other words, the first word in the sentence should begin with *s*, the second with *e*, the third with *n*, etc.

11. In one paragraph, describe a scene from any sport. Use these words somewhere in the paragraph:

bounced, struggled, spied, roared, collapsed, giggled (yes, *giggled!*).

12. Describe someone who looks bored. Don't use any form of the words *yawned* or *stared* or *sighed*.

13. Write one sentence consisting entirely of three-syllable words (not counting the articles *a*, *an*, and *the*).

14.
*New neighbors move in.
Something happens.
There is a confrontation.
They move out.*

Fill in the details so that this story is much more interesting.

15. As the writer for a clothing catalog, you must describe a sweater that is brown, beige, red-orange, and purple. Describe the sweater, but use new, two-word descriptions for each color. (Catalogs rarely describe something as *black*, for example. They are more likely to say *ebony ink* or *midnight oil*.) Be sure your description makes the sweater sound attractive.

16.

Writers can often tell something about a character by what the character says and how he says it.

For example, if a third grader walks into a classroom and says, with a little bow, "Good afternoon, Mr. Fendlehessey. I am extremely pleased to be attending your class today, and I wish you a successful and satisfying lesson," the reader knows that student is probably not your average, ordinary American child—at least not from this century.

Tell us something about the characters below through the words they use to say "no."

- A teenager in a heavy metal band turns down an offer to attend an opera with both grandparents.
- An older sibling refuses to play one more game of "Go Fish" with a little brother.
- A social media influencer who just received a manicure, a pedicure, and a new hairstyle turns down an offer to go fishing.

Now create an entirely different impression of the characters above by giving them different words.

Unjournaling © Taylor & Francis

17. Create a much more interesting version of this sentence:

The dog barked.

What kind of dog was it? Where was it? Why was it barking? How would you describe the barking? Make the sentence as interesting as possible by choosing your words and details carefully.

18. Here's what the artist called her painting:

Polar Bear Eating Vanilla Ice Cream in a Blizzard

To viewers, it looked like a plain white piece of canvas.
How might the same artist describe what looks like a plain blue canvas?
A plain red canvas?
A plain yellow canvas?

19. Like looking for a needle in a haystack
is a descriptive phrase that we have all heard. Create five different descriptive phrases that mean the same thing.

20.

Here's a bit of a story, told in two- and three-word sentences and phrases:

Bob cried. Elizabeth laughed. Sarah wondered why.
She asked. Elizabeth told her. "Bob lost."
"Lost what?"
"The bet."
"How much?"
"100 dollars"
"Ouch. He's crying. I see why."

Tell another bit of a story, using only two- and three-word sentences and phrases.

Unjournaling © Taylor & Francis.

21. Here's the last part of a newspaper story:

Neighbors called police when they noticed the pink gooey substance oozing from all the doors and windows of the modest ranch home.

Now write the first part of the story. Remember that a newspaper story starts right out answering the questions, "Who?," "What?," "Where?," "When?," "Why?," and "How?"

22. Brent told a joke. All five people in the room thought it was funny, though each one reacted differently. Describe the reactions of all five people.

23. Mr. and Ms. Pinehurst-Granola believe that school cheers are too violent. They don't like cheers like these:

*Hit 'em again.
Hit 'em again.
Harder! Harder!*

or

*Orange and black.
Sharks! Attack!*

To please the Pinehurst-Granolas, write a nice, gentle cheer for the Sharks.

24.

What advice would a DOG give about life, if it could talk? Write that advice.

25. What are the best reasons for doing nothing? List them.

26. Create an impression of a person, real or imaginary, by describing only the person's hands. Use only three sentences.

27. You are a writer who has a secret arrangement with the automobile industry. You will be paid $10.00 for every word you publish that includes the word *car*. (Examples: *scar cart, carp, carton.*) The hope is that repetition of the letters *c-a-r* will encourage people, subliminally, to want to buy cars.

You are starting a short story for a magazine. Write your first paragraph. How much money can you make using *c-a-r* in just that paragraph?

28. You have been hired for a special assignment: to design weird potato chip flavors that people might actually like. Think *Spicy Dill Pickle Potato Chips* or *Peanut Butter and Bacon Potato Chips.*

You have a big meeting coming up and you need to pitch five incredible and weirdly tasty ideas. What are the five special flavors? Write a description of one of them that will make it sound appealing.

29. Create a superhero for the Marvel Universe that specifically fits an over 65-years-old demographic. In approximately 200 words, give him or her a name, and describe the superhero's powers, look, and backstory.

30. Write a paragraph in which each word begins with a letter of the alphabet, in order backwards, from **Z** to **A**. (The first word will begin with **Z**, the second with **Y**, the next with **X**, etc.) You may use the articles *a*, *an*, and *the* wherever you wish.

31.

Write a three-sentence paragraph about a *dog*, using no letters of the alphabet that appear before "m."

---

32. Daunte's parents have very different communication styles. His dad is a poet who gives long and flowery requests. His mom is a major in the Air Force and gives short, straightforward orders. How does Daunte's dad tell him to wash the dishes? How does his mom communicate it? Write out the words of each.

33. There is smoke. Where is it coming from? You investigate and are surprised by what you find. Describe what you discover.

34. Write an "un-ad" that tells the absolute truth about a product.

35. Yazmin is looking back through the last year of her Instagram feed and is disappointed in all the boring things she has done. She is resolved to have more adventure in her life and is writing an adventure goal list. Help her dream up five wild antics that will crank up the adventure in her next year.

36. Some people can't smell. In one paragraph, make them understand "skunk."

37. *"When am I going to win the lottery?" asked Jenna.*

"When pigs fly," said Aaron.

Keeping the same meaning, write five different, more original responses for Aaron.

40. Chris walks into the room. By describing only the reactions of the others in the room, let us know something about Chris.

38.

Yankee Doodle went to town,
A-riding on a pony.
Stuck a feather in his cap
And called it "macaroni."

Why on earth would Yankee Doodle call his feather "macaroni"? Write a plausible explanation.

39. Write three different sentences, each using the word *crumpled*. Create an entirely different image with each sentence.

41. A child finds an extraterrestrial in her backyard. It is not like your average movie alien. Who is it? What is it like? What does the child do? What happens? Explain.

42. Take the words of a popular love song and alter them so that the song is no longer about love. For example, you might change the beginning of "I Will Always Love You" to "I Will Always Hate You." Or you might start a new version of "I Want to Hold Your Hand" with "I Want to Hold My Nose." Change the lyrics of the entire song.

43. Describe a car, using at least five comparisons to food. (Use color as a comparison no more than once.)

44.
In one sentence, communicate
"fear."

45.

A mother wants to be as positive as possible with her toddler. Here's what she needs to communicate:

- *We should not bonk other toddlers on the head with our Tonka truck.*

- *We should not throw Mommy's new shoes in the toilet.*

- *We should not draw elephants on the living room wall with crayons.*

How can she tell her child not to do these things, but in a positive way?

Unjournaling © Taylor & Francis

46. Write a sentence in which the first word is one letter long, the second word is two letters long, the third word is three letters long, etc. See how long you can make the sentence.

47. *Why? Why? Why?* A four-year-old wants to know *why* chairs have four legs. You explain that it is for balance. "Why else?" she asks. She won't stop asking "Why?" until you help her think of every reason imaginable.

List all the reasons you come up with, both serious and fanciful.

48. King Kong *stomped* along the street. He *crushed* cars with his toes. He *ripped* people from their cars. In five sentences, what else did he do? Use descriptive verbs.

49. You can use 25 words— no more—for a billboard advertising a new product called *Zebra Wink*. Sell your product with those 25 words.

50.   *Whine.*
            Bellyache.
            Complain.
            Moan.
            Criticize.

Create a conversation that uses some form of each of these words.

51.
Write an incredibly awesome paragraph about your absolute favorite actor, singer, or celebrity, using the most outstanding, excellent hyperbole in the whole, entire universe.

Hyperbole is extravagant exaggeration.

52.

Maddison whines—a lot. It's never about important things. It's always little things like this:

- My cell phone charger cord isn't long enough to reach the plug while I sit in bed. How am I supposed to charge and watch videos at the same time?
- My mom is always texting me. Why does she always have to bother me with stupid questions?
- I didn't get the two shots I asked for in my pumpkin spiced latte. What kind of barista leaves out the extra shot?

Write down five of Addison's recent whines.

53.

Hair. It can say a lot about a person. Create two very different characters in your mind. Use descriptions of their hair to tell us something about each.

54.

Lewis Carrol's famous poem "Jabberwocky" begins like this: "'Twas brillig and the slithy toves did gyre and gambol in the wabe."

Most of the words are nonsense words, but we still have an idea of what is going on. We know that *toves* are doing something. We know what they are doing. (They *did gyre* and *gambol*.) We know where all this is taking place: in the *wabe*.

The sentence fits the way we talk, even if the words have no meaning. *Toves* and *wabe* are nouns. *Gyre* and *gambol* are verbs. "Function" words like *the* and *and* and *in* hold everything together.

Just for the fun of it, try writing your own Jabberwocky sentence. Start with a real sentence. Then substitute nonsense words but keep the same sentence structure.

Example

Original sentence: *A determined fireman with an axe banged on the front door and hollered and hollered at us, trying to wake us.*

Jabberwocky sentence: *A lorgy fifflemont with a blort horgled and borgled at the flimey gix, trimping to malumph us.*

Now you try it. Start with the following sentence, and replace every word *except* the words that are in bold:

The angry monster **with a** hideous face stomped **and** clomped **to the** dark cave **where the** unsuspecting dragon slept.

55.

Write down ten clichés or phrases that you hear often. (She's as *cute as a button*. He's as *strong as an ox*. It was *pretty as a picture*.)

Show that you are as smart as a whip by writing a paragraph that includes as many of these clichés as possible.

56.

Now rewrite the paragraph you just wrote (#55), eliminating the clichés and substituting fresh descriptions.

57. An alien being from the planet Katzangorbia understands English but doesn't understand tattoos. The confused Katzangorbian wonders why many people have designs on different parts of their body. How did the designs get there? What are they good for? Help the Katzangorbian understand.

58. Pax is a very, very sensible person who doesn't believe in pretty, flowery, or romantic language. Write the letter Pax used to propose marriage.

59. People often say, *"If we can send a man to the moon, surely we can figure out how to…"* Complete the sentence five different ways.

60. Write a *rhyme* paragraph. Each sentence must begin and end with words that rhyme with each other.

An example:

Spring is a wonderful *thing. Flowers* start to sprout with the help of rain *showers.*

61. Take a line from a favorite song and a line from a favorite movie. Incorporate both quotes into a paragraph.

For example, you might combine the lines, "Somewhere over the rainbow," and "Make my day" and write, "I've looked everywhere for my favorite red sweater. I've looked in my closet, in my dresser, even under the furniture. I wonder where it could be? Perhaps it's *somewhere over the rainbow.* If you can help me find it, you will really *make my day!*"

62.
"Oh, please, don't sneeze!"
Write a paragraph that includes as many words as possible that rhyme with *sneeze.*

63. Tell a fish story.

Use as many *fishy* words as possible without actually writing about fish.

Examples of fishy words and phrases:

scales
whale of a good time
shrimp
clam up
net

64. Write about yesterday morning from the perspective of an everyday object or item—a salt shaker, a swing set, or a license plate, for example.

65. Write a *blue* paragraph, incorporating as many words that rhyme with the word *blue* as you possibly can.

66.

Poor Miss Shackleford has six-year-old Andrew Dunkle in her first grade class. In only three days, Andrew has caused Miss Shackleford to seriously consider resigning and becoming a waitress or a Chuck E. Cheese manager.

Miss Shackleford tries hard to see the good in every child and in every situation. She doesn't really believe that little Andrew has the potential to become an ax murderer, despite what he did to the goldfish.

Help Miss Shackleford write an email to Mr. and Mrs. Dunkle, accentuating the positive but letting them know that Andrew needs to learn just a tad more self-discipline.

67. Pen a paragraph that is permeated with *p*s. In other words, write a paragraph that uses at least ten alliterative phrases that repeat the *p* sound.

Alliteration is the repetition of consonant sounds. Example:

Bob boiled beans with a bunch of broccoli and bits of bacon.

68.
Write a paragraph or a poem about *winter*, **starting every sentence or line with the letter** *W*. Only one can start with the word *winter*.

69. Write a five-sentence paragraph of five-letter words (not counting *a*, *an*, or *the*.) Make the subject of your paragraph an animal.

70. List ten words that use *ph* to make an *f* sound. (Example: *phrase*.)

Then use all ten words in a paragraph.

71.
Keenan has written a book.
It's called *Slithering Secrets*. He is self-publishing it, so he needs to write the "blurb" describing the book for Amazon.com. Help him out by writing the description of his novel. Make it sound as inviting as possible.

72. Write a paragraph with at least nine words that start with the letter *a* and include nine letters.

73. Write a paragraph that starts with this sentence:

The grass smells red.

74. Use a thesaurus to look up synonyms for the word *befuddled.* Choose seven synonyms, and write a sentence using each. Make each sentence as different as possible from the others.

75. Most people believe *vomit* is an ugly word. Write a paragraph that incorporates at least ten words *you* believe are ugly.

76. Write a conversation between two people, making the conversation consist entirely of questions.

Example:

"Do you want to grab a hamburger?" asked Chris.
"Do vegetarians eat beef now?" asked Amber.

See how long you can make the conversation.

77. "Yipes," said the zebra. "I've lost my stripes." Continue the paragraph, using as many words as you possibly can that rhyme with *yipes.*

78. Write a paragraph about *summer* that does *not* use the letter *s.*

79.

Write a paragraph about a toddler eating her first piece of birthday cake—but without using these words:

sticky, gooey, messy.

80. Burp! Slosh! Snort! Write a paragraph incorporating at least ten onomatopoetic words.

Onomatopoetic words are words that sound like what they mean. Examples:

beep
boing
swoosh
hiccup
plop
fizz

81. **Rewrite "Mary Had a Little Lamb"** so that Mary has a new animal, and she's taking it somewhere other than to school. In case you need a reminder of the words, here they are:

Mary had a little lamb,
Little lamb, little lamb.
Mary had a little lamb.
Its fleece was white as snow.

Everywhere that Mary went,
Mary went, Mary went.
Everywhere that Mary went,
The lamb was sure to go.

It followed her to school one day,
School one day, school one day.
It followed her to school one day,
Which was against the rules.

It made the children laugh and play,
Laugh and play, laugh and play.
It made the children laugh and play
To see a lamb at school.

82. Bippity-boppity- boo! Create your own fairy godmother. What does she look like? What does she have to offer you? Explain how she helps you. Describe her personality.

83.
Write a three-sentence paragraph about the view out an apartment window, without using the word "the."

84. Write ten food and people similes. In other words, compare a person (real or imagined) to food. For example, you might say, "Franco is as assertive as a wilted piece of lettuce," or, "Marianna's hair is as red as tomato soup." Your comparisons should create a very clear image of the person.

85. Finish this sentence three different ways, creating a different feeling with each sentence:

As Antonio opened the door, he gasped to see . . .

86. Write a three-sentence paragraph using only the first half of the alphabet, letters *a-l.* (You may not use *t, m, s* or any other letter that appears past *l* in the alphabet.)

87. Describe something bland in one sentence that really makes a reader feel how bland it is.

88. Only a handful of words in the English dictionary start with *dw.* Here are three:

dwell
dwindle
dweeb

Write a paragraph that incorporates all three of these *dw* words. (Feel free to invent a few new *dw* words to add to your paragraph.)

89. Austin's mother sings too much. She sings while doing laundry. She sings while making dinner. She sings while driving to work. Worst of all, she sings when she is driving Austin and his friends to their soccer games or to the mall.

Describe a typical car ride with Austin, his friends, and his mother. What is his mother singing? How does she sound? What is Austin doing? What are his friends doing? Create a picture of the scene, in words.

Unjournaling © Taylor & Francis

90.

Some ideas are just bad ideas. Trying to touch a bison in the wild is a bad idea. Buying a pet mouse when you already have a pet boa constrictor is a bad idea. Washing your red shirt with your white underwear is a bad idea. Using your hand to unclog a running garbage disposal is a bad idea.

List ten more extremely bad ideas.

91.

The answer is, "No."
What is the question?

The answer is, "Yes."
What is the question?

The answer is, "Maybe."
What is the question?

The answer is, "What is the question?"
What is the question?

92. "Oops," muttered Miss Klinkfelder.

Why the "Oops"? Describe what led up to Miss Klinkfelder's "Oops."

93. Fatima is a very spoiled teenage girl. Show that she is spoiled, without saying she is spoiled, by describing what happens when she doesn't get a car for her birthday.

94. *"You're pulling my leg!"* is an expression that has nothing to do with real legs. Write an explanation that describes how the expression originated. (Since, of course, you probably have no idea, your explanation will be pulling the leg of anyone who reads it!)

95. Write about an argument. Make each sentence start with the last letter of the previous sentence. (If the first sentence ends in an *e*, the next sentence should start with an *e*.)

96. What's *icky?* Write five sentences describing five *icky* things.

97.

Have you ever had a leg cramp? If so, you are in luck. There are countless cures for leg cramps. Here are just some of the "cures" many believe will stop a leg cramp:

- *Eat a teaspoon of yellow mustard.*
- *Lick salt off your hand.*
- *Pinch the skin between your nose and your mouth.*
- *Sleep with a bar of soap in your bed.*

While these certainly sound impossible many people swear that they work. Invent an impossible sounding cure for leg cramps, hiccups, mosquito bites, or warts. Write a paragraph convincing people that this cure is amazingly true. You may want to include "quotes" from a person or doctor who has used your cure. You may want to include a so-called "scientific" explanation for why your cure works.

98. Only the best is good enough for Bartholomew. (Never call him Bart!) Describe a typical evening for him.

99. What if the sky were not blue, but red? List five effects this would have on everyday life.

100.

Sylvia McDaniel is still reeling from the breakup with her most recent boyfriend, who was what she liked to call *adjective impaired.*

He was always choosing the wrong adjectives. He called her hair *frizzy*, while she would have preferred *wavy*. He called her *bony*, while she would have preferred *slim*. He called her family *weird*, while she would have preferred *eccentric*.

He also described her beloved dog like this:

That squat little mutt has a frumpy haircut. It is blobby. It has stumpy legs. It is yappy, fussy, ill-behaved, and annoying.

Rewrite his description of the dog as it might sound if he were *not* adjective impaired.

101.
Unbeknownst to most people, the chicken had *a lot* of reasons for crossing the road. What were at least five of them?

102. The young person known as the *Queen of Cute* has a new puppy. This puppy is very pampered. How does the Queen of Cute describe this new little darling?

103. You know what an *orfinbellydorper* is. Most people don't. Explain to them what to do with one.

104.

Alyssa's writing teacher says that her writing is too choppy, with many short sentences that could be combined. She also suggests that Alyssa could organize her work more sensibly.

For example, Alyssa wrote this paragraph:

I like to play with my dog. She likes to play catch with a stuffed squeaky toy. It is a rubber raccoon. My dog is a poodle. Her name is Cocoa. She was a gift from my grandfather. He gave her to me on my eleventh birthday. She has been my best friend ever since. She trots beside me on my morning runs. I wish I could take her to school. Dogs aren't allowed there, of course. She sits at my feet when I'm eating. She curls up beside me when I watch TV. She sleeps at the foot of my bed. I take good care of my dog. I feed her only high-quality dog food. I give her lots of attention.

Unjournaling © Taylor & Francis

She likes to go to the park with me. There she chases Frisbees. I love her a lot. I love her more than my cell phone. I love my cell phone a lot. I groom Cocoa daily.

Her teacher suggested that one way to rewrite the paragraph would be like this:

I like to play with my poodle, Cocoa. My grandfather gave her to me as a gift on my eleventh birthday, and she has been my best friend ever since. She trots beside me on my morning runs, sits at my feet when I'm eating, curls up beside me when I watch TV, and sleeps at the foot of my bed. I would take her to school with me if I could, but dogs aren't allowed. I take good care of Cocoa, feeding her only high-quality dog food, grooming her daily, and giving her lots of attention. She loves to go to the park with me and chase Frisbees. She also loves to play catch with a stuffed squeaky toy, a rubber raccoon. I love Cocoa even more than my cell phone, and I love my cell phone a lot.

Here is another one of Alyssa's paragraphs. Rewrite it so that is less choppy and organize it more sensibly.

I have to walk past a creepy building every day. It is on the way to school. The building is four stories tall. The windows are boarded over. Some people think the building is haunted. The doors are boarded over. Once I even heard a yipping sound coming from inside. Most of the paint has worn off the building. The porch has rotted boards. It has holes in it, too. Strange lights appear inside at night. What kind of building yips? Strange sounds come from there, too. Moaning sometimes. Screams sometimes. Whistles. I get goosebumps whenever I am near it. I always cross the street. I walk on the other side. I want to avoid the creepy building.

105. Write a very, very, very long question, with a very, very, very short couplet for an answer. (A couplet is simply two lines that rhyme.)

Example:

What did Mr. Elwin say when his wife locked him out of the house for coming home late when he was supposed to stay home that night and take her out to dinner for their anniversary, which he forgot?

*Move over,
Rover.*

106. Write another very, very, very long question with a very, very, very short couplet for an answer.

107. Complete the following ten different ways: *"Never . . ."*

108.

*Jack and Jill went up the hill
To fetch a pail of water.
Jack fell down and broke his crown,
And Jill came tumbling after.*

There is too much left out of this story. Who were Jack and Jill? How did they go up that hill? Did they walk? Ride a horse? Drive in a car? Why did they need a pail of water? Why didn't they just turn on a faucet? What made Jack fall down? How far did he fall? How serious was his "crown" injury? What made Jill tumble? Was she hurt?

Rewrite the story, filling in details to tell us what really happened.

Unjournaling © Taylor & Francis

109. Oddly enough, many *unk* words suggest something unpleasant. Write an unpleasant paragraph using the words *drunk, dunk, junk, skunk, stunk,* and *gunk.*

110. When Sam is really mad, he rants. He carries on and on about what is wrong, but without using any profanity. Sam is mad again. Write what he says in his rant.

111. List three tactful but true things a person might say about Aunt Krissie's awful beet juice and lima bean Jell-O salad.

112. Shoot the moon. Write a story that includes 20 "oo" words.

113. Olivia has been criticized by her boyfriend for not expressing her feelings enough. "I never know what you think about anything!" he says. "You never give me any details. You shut me out of your thoughts and your life!"

Olivia decides to teach him a lesson. When he comes to pick her up one night, she shares, completely, every detail and thought in her head from the time they leave the house until they get in the car and shut the door. What does she say?

114.
Write four sentences made up of four four-letter words each.

115. Different groups often use slang that others don't understand. A teenaged skateboarder may use slang that is baffling to his parents. A grandparent may use slang that sounds silly to her grandchildren. The kitchen staff in a café may use slang that a soccer mom wouldn't understand. Computer geeks use slang that only other computer geeks understand.

Write a paragraph about a movie or a concert, using as much slang as possible. (You choose the kind of slang.) Be sure to overdo it!

116. Everyone in the group knew better than to say, "How are you?" to Mildred. Once again, though, someone forgot.

Write down Mildred's lengthy response.

117. Here's what William hopes:

He sincerely hopes that, with time and patience and firm but gentle guidance and love, his daughter Angelica, who has insisted upon being called "Cobra Girl" ever since she got the tattoo down the left side of her neck, will have someone besides the police escort her home sometimes. He hopes she might start volunteering at the nursing home again and maybe even get a job, using that high school diploma of hers for something besides a liner in her sock drawer.

Tell what Cobra Girl has in mind.

Unjournaling © Taylor & Francis

118.
Write a four-line song
or poem about
mayonnaise.

119. It was a great truck, a fantastic truck, the truck of Carter's dreams. No one had ever seen a truck like it. It made Carter so happy.

Describe the truck.

120. In writing, show that a room has a very, very bad smell—but without saying it has a very, very bad smell.

121. Your life may depend on it. You're a spy. You're in danger. You have to get off an island, fast. You have arranged a signal with the owner of a boat. If he receives a note inviting him to a party, but without using the letter *a*, he knows to come for you, fast. To avoid suspicion if the note is intercepted, you want to be sure and include all the details about the party, including the reason for it.

Write your note. Be careful, though. One accidental *a* means you won't be rescued!

122.
You are paying $10.00 per word to advertise in the online classified section of the *Upscale Times*, a newspaper for a very wealthy area. You want to offer your services as a dog sitter.

Write a convincing ad, but don't spend more than $200.00.

123.

Everyone hates it when Uncle Milhouse tells a story. It's not that his stories are bad—or at least they wouldn't be if he would just stick to the story. The problem is, he wanders. He'll say something like:

> Back in 1972, you wouldn't believe the tornado that hit our town. That was the year my dad got laid off at the factory...the pickle factory, it was. They were called Fickle Pickles, and they were the best darn dills you ever ate. Well, maybe my grandma's were just a tad better, to tell you the truth. She said her secret was to add a little cinnamon to the jars. Now, my wife, your Aunt Letitia, she says that's nonsense, that you can't add cinnamon to pickles, but, well, Grandma insisted that's what she did. Grandma was kind of known for her odd ideas. She could have put cinnamon in her pickles. I know for a fact that she put vinegar in her cherry pies, and they sure were good. It was probably because the cherries were fresh. She picked them straight off the tree in her backyard—the tree that got knocked over when a truck landed on it in 1972. It was during that gosh-awful tornado we had, and that truck, it just...

You get the idea. How does Uncle Milhouse tell the story of what happened when his sister tried to elope with a used car salesman?

124. Kaitlyn's mommy has a tendency to overuse the word *awesome*. If Kaitlyn drinks her milk, her mother says, "Awesome!" If her dad asks Kaitlyn to hand him the remote control, and she does, her mother says, "Awesome!" If Kaitlyn puts one tiny blue dot on a piece of paper and says, "It's a tree, Mommy!" her mother says, "Awesome!"

Kaitlyn and her mother are going to the supermarket this morning. Write a paragraph describing their trip to the store, incorporating Kaitlyn's mommy's favorite word.

125. Write a paragraph on a subject of your choice, using only one-syllable words.

126. Here's the beginning of a paragraph:

Quenton felt queasy after eating quince and quail.

Finish the paragraph, using as many *qu* words as possible. Try for at least ten.

127.

Mac is a person who loves himself. He loves himself very, very, very much.

Show how much Mac thinks of himself by describing some of his actions, in one paragraph. Describe only his actions, not his thoughts.

128. Mr. and Mrs. Alfredo Wilkowitz named their son **Hokey Pokey Wilkowitz.** Not surprisingly, Hokey wants to know what they were thinking. Explain for them, clearly but kindly.

129. The answer is *mouthwash*. What is the question? Write five possible questions for that answer. (Try for originality— something more than, "What can I use to freshen my breath?")

130. Newspaper writers are supposed to be concise and stick to the facts. Marcella Romano has been criticized for being too concise. For example, she turned in this story last week:

There was a fight yesterday on Main Street at 1:00 a.m. It was a bad one.

Fill in the details for Marcella.

131.

Write a paragraph that starts with this sentence:

Why can't we just get some tattoos or something?

End your paragraph with this sentence:

The ring maker will be here in 10 minutes.

Unjournaling © Taylor & Francis

132. Penelope wants to close her restaurant. It is very successful, but she has to work long, long hours, and she is tired.

Her husband, however, doesn't want her to close it. He likes all the money it brings in, and he can be very cranky and hard to live with when he doesn't get his way.

Penelope decides the answer is to *cause* her business to be less successful, so that she will eventually have to close it. She starts by replacing three popular items on the menu each week with three dreadful entreés.

To help her out, name three new menu items for her, and write a short description of each. Remember, it's important to Penelope that her restaurant *fails*.

133.

Write an original tongue twister.

Some ideas:

- Use a lot of words that start with and/or include the same letter, as in *Peter Piper Picked a Peck of Pickled Peppers*.

- Or use a lot of words that are very similar to each other, like *group* and *goop* or *spot* and *slot*.

---

134. Write a sentence with every single word beginning with either *a* or *t*.

135. In one sentence, describe something (not someone) that is *very ugly*. Create a vividly ugly image, with words.

136.

Write a letter to an animal, creating a very clear mood with the tone of your letter. Are you going to address your dog? The neighbor's dog? A fish at the dentist's office? A lobster in a tank at a seafood restaurant? A penguin at the zoo? Think about why you are writing to this animal—to save it from being a fur coat, to threaten a lawsuit if it doesn't stop its constant barking during "Survivor"? Are you going to be serious? Silly? Whimsical? Funny? Or…?

137. The accused stood before the court and said, "Mistakes were made," and "I'm sorry for what happened."

"The way he puts it, you'd hardly guess that he had anything to do with that burglary," muttered the woman whose store he broke into.

Rewrite the accused's words, to more accurately reflect what really happened.

138.

Here's your chance to break the rules. See how many adjectives you can use in a paragraph to tell us as little as possible about a person walking into a party and catching everyone's eye. Choose vague adjectives that don't really help create a picture. (Adjectives, to refresh your memory, are words that describe nouns. Examples of boring adjectives: a *nice* boy, a *good* time, a *happy* baby.)

139. Now do the opposite of what you just did in item #138. Take the same paragraph and replace the boring adjectives with more interesting adjectives. Examples: *agitated* alligator, *slimy* bowl of soup, *stone-aged* computer with a *pea-sized* hard drive.

Unjournaling © Taylor & Francis

140.

"The letter was sent" is a passive sentence.
"Hank sent the letter" is an active sentence.

"The game was won by us" is passive.
"We won the game" is active.

"I am loved" is passive.
"Alfred loves me" is active.

Active sentences have someone performing the action in the sentence, instead of receiving it. They are almost always much stronger than passive sentences.

Try your hand at improving the following passive description of a car accident. Rewrite it so that all the sentences are active.

> The semi truck was plowed into by a PT Cruiser that was driven by a middle-aged former hippie who is still sad about having to give up his Volkswagen bus. The PT Cruiser was ruined by the impact. The former hippie was taken to the hospital by an ambulance. The ambulance was driven by a show-off taking his first turn at driving. The ambulance was driven too fast by him, and it was hit by a Porsche when a red light was ignored by both him and the Porsche driver—a five-foot tall grandmother of twelve who was eager to get to the dance at the Eagles Club. All the wrecks were survived by all the people involved.

141. Add one sentence that completely changes the impression this description makes:

The new teacher sitting at her desk slowly looked up at the class. She cleared her throat carefully several times and then, in a voice so soft the students could barely hear her, said, "Excuse me. Excuse me." Students giggled a bit and kept right on talking.

142. Great-grandpa Rotondo doesn't understand what a video game is. Or an iPad. Or text messaging.

Pick one of the above— or any other technological invention or process that wasn't around when Great-grandpa was younger. Explain what it is in terms that even the most un-technological person can understand.

143. The letters *tion* are very common at the end of English nouns. Here are just a few:

station, nation, anticipation, flirtation, vacation, combination, expectation, centralization, regurgitation.

Write a four-line poem in which each line ends in a *tion* word. (If you're on a roll, go ahead and make the poem longer than four lines.)

144. Somebody's sitting behind you on the bus. You hear only one side of an odd cell phone conversation, but it is intriguing and alarms you.
What do you hear?

Unjournaling © Taylor & Francis

145. What would blue taste like

if you could chew it?

. . . . . .

146.

Abraham Lincoln's famous first sentence from the Gettysburg Address is "Fourscore and seven years ago our fathers brought forth on this continent, a new nation, conceived in liberty and dedicated to the proposition that all men are created equal." Copy the form of the sentence as much as possible, but update the subject matter to note a wedding, a birth, or some other "event."

For example, instead of saying "Fourscore and seven years ago," you might begin your sentence with "Two years and seven months ago..."

Try three different updates.

147. What if the shape *round* did not exist, except as the shape of the earth and moon?

Looking at just your immediate world, how would your life be different?

148. Write a sentence (or more than one sentence) about celebrating a holiday. Use exactly 100 letters—no more, no less.

149.
Create a *super hero* that the world needs. Your super hero must be entirely original, unlike any super hero you know of who has ever been created before.

What special powers does the hero have? What problem will he or she solve for the world, or for a certain population of the world? Will the hero solve a really important problem, or just a smaller, annoying problem?

150.
Use all five vowels (a, e, i, o, u) at least once in a sentence about *gravy.*

151. Madison is so *happy*. In one paragraph, show that she is happy, but don't use the word *happy* or even a synonym for *happy*.

152. Write a sentence with no "ascenders" or "descenders." Ascenders or descenders are letters that have parts that extend above or below the main part of the letter in most type fonts: *b, d, f, g, h, i, j, k, l, p, q, t, y.* (Capital letters don't count.)

Unjournaling © Taylor & Francis

153. Here are the letters you can use:

e, s, a, t, r, c, n, m, h, w, d.

How many sentences can you write, using only these letters?

154. Write a short conversation that might take place between two people who are unlikely ever to meet. For example, you might have LeBron James talk to Benjamin Franklin or Lin-Manuel Miranda talk to King Tut. You might write a conversation between your third grade teacher and Ariana Grande, or Simone Biles and the guy at the end of your street who seems to be collecting bird baths and old tires.

155.

Jasmine was bored at work, so she wrote an email to her best friend Erin, telling all about the *stupid* things her boss had done that day. Just as she finished, the phone rang. As she picked up the phone, she accidentally hit "Eric" instead of "Erin" in her address book. Eric is her boss.

Jasmine decided never ever to go to work again.

What on earth did she write? (Note: She did not swear.)

156. How many different ways can you say that precipitation fell—without actually using the words "*Precipitation fell***"?**

157. Write a fake news story that includes the following words:

tater tot casserole
zipper
geraniums
karate.

158.

Three people are stuck in an elevator:

- a teenager with green hair and many body piercings
- a pastry chef
- a church organist.

Write the conversation they have as they wait.

---

159. Write a paragraph consisting of only *six letter words* (not counting *a, an,* or *the*).

160. You have undoubtedly heard the children's song, "Here We Go 'Round the Mulberry Bush." Explain why they might be going around a mulberry bush.

161.

"I request some money." Rewrite this sentence as each of the people listed below might word it. For each person, set the scene with one sentence. Then tell what the person said.

- A teenager to a parent.
- A bank robber to a teller.
- A woman to her ex-husband.
- A couple to a loan officer at a bank.
- A policeman to a driver.
- A dissatisfied customer to a store owner.
- A man who walked into a glass door to the concierge.

Unjournaling © Taylor & Francis

162. Write a short essay or story that includes 26 sentences. The first sentence must begin with the letter A, the second sentence with B, the third with C and so on, until you have used the entire alphabet.

163. "I wouldn't marry you even if you were the last man on earth," said Nadine.

Jeremy just smiled. He thought she was kidding.

She wasn't.

Help Nadine get through to Jeremy by completing the following sentence five different ways:

*I
wouldn't
marry
you
if...*

164. Write a three-sentence paragraph with every word beginning with the letter *s* (except for the articles *a*, *an*, and *the*).

165.

They say opposites attract. Use at least five pairs of opposites in a paragraph about some kind of transportation.

Examples:

*weak/strong
loud/quiet
high/low.*

166. A person's choice of a pet is said to express something about his or her personality. Choose five individuals whose names are well-known nationally. What kind of pet would you choose for each? Why? Explain.

167. Write a paragraph that starts with a *one-word sentence*, followed by a *two-word sentence*, then a *three-word sentence*, then a *four-word sentence*, etc.

How far can you go? Can you get as high as ten sentences?

168. Florencia wants a cat.

Her mother doesn't want her to have one. "However," her mother said, "I can be persuaded if your arguments are good enough. Write a convincing paragraph that will make me change my mind."

Forencia changed her mind. What did she write?

169.

Write a paragraph describing a place to eat. Use every letter of the alphabet at least once.

170.

Here's the title of a poem:

OMG!

Write the poem.

171. Farley and Filmore run into each other at a party. It is clear they can't stand each other, even though neither one says a word, and neither one gets violent.

Write a paragraph describing what happens.

Unjournaling © Taylor & Francis

172. Write a paragraph that starts and ends with the word *computer*.

173.

The Bulwer-Lytton Fiction Contest is held every year to recognize the author of the worst possible opening line for a book. To enter, contestants simply submit the worst sentence they can imagine to begin a book.

The contest is in "honor" of Edward George Bulwer-Lytton, who began a book in 1830 with this long sentence: *It was a dark and stormy night; the rain fell in torrents—except at occasional intervals, when it was checked by a violent gust of wind which swept up the streets (for it is in London that our scene lies), rattling along the housetops, and fiercely agitating the scanty flame of the lamps that struggled against the darkness.*

Try your hand at writing a really bad sentence for the contest.

174.

Describe someone who is making a fashion statement, whatever that statement might be.

175.

Write a paragraph about apple pie without using the letters *a* or *p*.

176. Give ten useful pieces of advice to a specific person or group, beginning each piece of advice with *"Always…"* For example, you might consider advice to your child or your future child, advice to a parent, advice to a teacher, or advice to the President of the United States.

177. You've heard this expression:

Woe is me.

Address a different situation:

Woe is Joe.

Write Joe's melodramatic description of his woes. (Or write *Jo's* melodramatic description of *her* woes.)

178. Why does it snow? Why do we have earthquakes? Why do leaves turn brown? Write a farfetched explanation of any natural phenomenon. For example, you could explain how rain is a result of the sun sweating because of the excessive heat.

179.
Write a paragraph that shows a stereotypical character doing something stereotypical. Examples:

A weightlifter looks around to be sure people are watching, then does some muscle flexing and stretching in front of the mirror.

The librarian glares at the children laughing at one of the tables and says, "Shhhhhhhh!"

Then go back and change one sentence so that your character is no longer stereotypical—and much more interesting to the reader.

Unjournaling © Taylor & Francis

180.

Write a news paragraph that includes the following words:

cantaloupe, toothpaste, guitar, flashlight, flip-flops.

181. *Invent new words.*

Choose a six-letter word. Add a letter to invent a new, original word. Define this word.

Now, change one letter in your new word to create another new word. Define this word.

Use the original word and both of the new words in a paragraph.

182. Prepositions are those little words that we don't pay much attention to but use all the time. Just a few examples:

of, into, at, by, to, up, on, by, in.

Write a paragraph about the final moments of a tied basketball game *or* someone's encounter with a used car salesman at a dealership—*without* using any of the prepositions just mentioned.

183. Make up a fake name by combining a random first name and random last name from the Internet. Create a character based on the sound of this name. Reveal something about the character by describing him or her going into a restaurant for dinner.

184. You can tell a lot about a person by what he or she says. Here are some things Grandma Dorothy always says:

"You can never be too dressed up."

"A woman should never ask a man to dance."

"He is quite a snappy dresser."

Based on these sentences, imagine what kind of person Grandma Dorothy is. Write a paragraph describing her. Feel free to use any or all of her quotations.

185. You've heard song parodies such as *On Top of Spaghetti* (to the tune of "On Top of Old Smoky"). Perhaps you have listened to Weird Al Yankovich's parodies like *Lasagna* (to the tune of "La Bamba"). Or perhaps you have heard the singing group Capitol Steps, which performs parodies like *God Bless My SUV* (To the tune of "God Bless the USA").

Write your own parody of a well-known song, either an old standard or something more recent.

186.

For five years, *Webster's New International Dictionary* included an entry for the word *dord*. However, *dord* is not an actual word. (Even dictionary makers can make mistakes!) Invent your own definition for the word.

Write a paragraph using your newly defined word.

187.

Dictionary Diving. Open your dictionary or use an online random word generator and select a word that a person would not normally use in conversation. (Don't choose a capitalized word.) Include that word in a paragraph.

If you are feeling really brave, dictionary dive five times and select five unusual words to incorporate into one paragraph.

> # 188.
> Choose a fictional or real-life character. How would he or she react in a crisis?
> Imagine that your character's car has broken down in an unfamiliar area of the city. Write a description of your character's reaction.

189.

In English, writers generally use *ah-choo* to describe the sound made by a sneeze. In Russian, the sound is *ap-chi*. In Chinese it is *han-chee*. In Czechoslovakian, it is *kychnuti*. Create five more ways to describe the sound a sneeze makes.

Then use them all in a paragraph about someone with allergies.

190. Imagine you are the newest employee of Rumors, Inc., and your sole job is to write clever hoax email stories that people will believe. Write a story that is just crazy enough to be true—one that would be believable to the millions of people who forward crazy-sounding email stories.

Here are a few sample ideas:

- Beware of thieves using boxes of corn flakes to steal your identity.

- Dog lovers, beware. Cats can cause some breeds of dogs to stop eating forever.

- Guard your earlobes! Outbreaks of earlobe theft have been reported in all major U.S. cities over the past six months.

191.

Place this sentence in a paragraph where it will make sense:

Bea had never before wanted to be a bee.

192. Some say you can tell a lot about a person by the vehicle he or she drives. **Picture a car.** (Or is it a truck? Or an SUV?)

In your mind, rummage through this car. Check it out from every angle.

Describe the car and the person who goes with it.

Unjournaling © Taylor & Francis

193.

You are dressing for the ostentatious Met Gala and the theme is Dystopian Sunshine. What do you wear? Describe your jaw-dropping outfit.

194.

Euphemisms are polite words for something unpleasant. For example, we often say *passed on* instead of *died* or *kicked the bucket*.

New neighbors have just moved in, and they are asking who lives in the house on the corner. It's Arnold, the weirdest guy in the neighborhood. Describe Arnold to them, being truthful, but using euphemisms to describe his bizarre behavior.

195.

Allegorical names generally give a hint about who a character is. *Herman Pocketprotector* might be a nerd, for example, or *Hazel Scuttlebutt* a busybody.

Invent two characters with allegorical names. Then write a conversation between them. What they say should reflect the personality suggested by their names.

196.

Write a paragraph that starts with this sentence:

Why don't you learn how to talk to a rooster?

and ends with this one:

She slugged him.

197. Create a character named *Pat.* Who is Pat? You are creating this person, so you decide.

How old is Pat? Who does Pat live with? What disappoints Pat? What recently made Pat unhappy? How unhappy? What does Pat like to do on Sunday afternoons?

Using what you know about Pat so far, describe Pat's meeting with *someone else* about *something, somewhere.*

198. How many ways can you find to communicate, in writing, *"He has a strong body"*—without actually writing, *"He has a strong body"*?

199. Songs for little children sometimes leave a lot to be desired. For example, *Rock-a-Bye Baby* has a baby falling out of a tree. *Little Bunny Foo Foo* has a bunny picking up mice and "boppin' 'em on the head."

Write a more cheerful and wholesome song for children, using the tunes of the above-mentioned songs or creating your own tune.

200.
Describe the personality of a group that has a personality. It can be a real group or an imaginary group.

Is it a club? A team? A clique? A class at a school? The people who hang out at a certain restaurant or coffee shop? What kind of personality does the group have?

Unjournaling © Taylor & Francis

201. Google was originally called *BackRub*. Imagine if the name had stuck. We'd now hear things like, "I never heard of a red-nosed batfish. Let me grab my phone and backrub it."

Pepsi was originally named *Brad's Drink*. Of course that was in 1893. The creator, Caleb Bradham, changed the name five years later.

Jeff Bezos wanted to call Amazon *Cadabra*. Reportedly, someone misheard the name and thought it was *Cadaver*. He decided to rethink the name.

Kai has a good idea for a company. Unfortunately, no one thinks the name is a good idea. Write a description of Kai's good idea, and then come up with a better name. (Google the name to make sure it's not already taken.)

202. The letters *ough* can be pronounced many different ways. For example, look at the following words:

Cough (*aw*)
Rough (*uh*)
Dough (*oh*)

Write a short rhyming poem with lines that end in these words.

203.

Venec's great-grandmother keeps posting strange stories on social media sites, and they always, *always* tell of an injury from performing an everyday task. For example, yesterday she told a complicated story that ended with this warning: Don't lose a toe making your bed! (She has 153 likes.)

What happened that resulted in the loss of a toe? Fill in the details.

204. Maxmillian Mariano Mancini married Melissa Macduff. They named their children Montague, Meryl, Myron, and Missie. Their dog is Mutty. Their cat is Muffin.

Describe the Mancini home, using as many "m" words as possible in your description.

205. "It must be easy to create a podcast," thought Quinn, a person not known for modesty. "All I need is a microphone and a topic I can talk about."

Quinn looked through a list of podcasts and found one called "Stuff You Should Know." That gave him an idea. "I'm going to do a podcast called *Stuff I Already Know That You Should Know, Too*, and give my advice. People will love my wisdom."

Here are Quinn's topics for the first three episodes:

Smart Ways to Get Out of Stuff
Things I Do That You
    Should Copy
Why You Should Give Me Money

Choose one of the topics and write a *summary* of what that episode will include. Don't write the whole episode. Just summarize the main points.

206.

While eating a giant bowl of Frooty Loops, Ursula was listening to a podcast about UFO encounters. Something suddenly happened. She woke up with a milk mustache, a spoon in her back pocket, and a strange otherworldly feeling. Describe what might have happened to Ursula, using the letters U, F, and O at least ten times each.

Unjournaling © Taylor & Francis

207.

Garvey loves gravy. He loves it so much that he opened a restaurant called Good Gravy, incorporating gravy into every item on the menu. Customers get a choice of brown or white gravy, and they love it on things like hot turkey sandwiches or fries. Nobody, however, is ordering the pancakes with gravy, gravy soda, milkshake, or lemon meringue pie à la gravy.

Garvey desperately needs your help. Good Gravy will have to close if he does not start selling some of the unpopular gravy specialties. He has hired you to write a 30-second radio spot that will surely convince the public to try these gravy concoctions. (A 30-second radio spot contains up to 90 words.)

208.

Stella and Cosmo are twins. While they both have an undying love for the song "Jolene" by Dolly Parton, they have wildly different tastes in music. Stella loves songs that are happy and upbeat; Cosmo loves music that is slow and moody. How would they describe each other's music taste? Write a short paragraph for each person from their twin's perspective, including examples of songs.

209. Dario has a secret. He loves to load and unload the dishwasher. In fact, he hates when other people do it because they don't do it right. Rather than cringing while his mom and stepbrother do it wrong, he has decided to write a dishwashing manual that can't be traced back to him. (His family is more likely to follow the "rules" if they don't know he wrote them.) What are ten guidelines Dario might include in his dishwasher manual?

210.

Like many successful people, billionaire Philmore Kranz claims that his morning routine is part of what makes him so successful. He wakes up at 4:00 a.m., meditates, takes a cold shower, and eats exactly seven turkey sausages—and that's only part of his routine.

Lola Lopez is an entrepreneur with nearly a billion dollars in sales. Newspapers everywhere are clamoring to hear what she does every morning that helps make her so successful. Describe Lola's morning routine, accounting for four full hours of what she admits is "unusual" morning behavior. Include anything she does on a daily basis, including meals, exercise, social media posts, etc.

211.

Thousands of new words in the English language are created every year. It's your turn to create one. Come up with a new word to describe each of the following:

- being bent over a cell phone
- texting rapidly with the thumbs
- some other action

Make sure each word is pronounceable, and google it to be sure someone hasn't already come up with it. (You may be surprised to learn how many supposedly new words aren't new at all.)

When you have the words, write a sentence for each that illustrates its use and suggests its meaning.

212.

One little mistake can sometimes lead to surprising outcomes. Crossing a busy city street, Hoshi dropped her cell phone. Explain how that led to fish dying on the carpet.

213. Compare three different animals to things you plug in. How are they alike?

214. Yusuf is a baker who writes a blog about his work and attracts a surprising number of subscribers. However, for reasons known only to him, he hate, hate, *hates* the letter B. Write a blog entry for him, telling about the new recipes he has come up with for brownies, bread, and bagels—but without using the letter B. He will be selling all three at an upcoming street festival, and anyone who stops at his booth can have a free taste.

215. Three people at a get-together are silent, each for a different reason. One is embarrassed. One is angry. One is bored.

Describe each of these people so that we understand what they are feeling, even though they are silent.

216. The two-foot tall creature emerged from the space ship that landed in the middle of a busy city street. What did it look like? Do not use any synonyms for *short* or *ugly*.

217. Manuel enters a contest where the prize is $100 for every "R" used in a paragraph of 100 words or less. He wins the contest. What did his paragraph say?

218.

Think outside the box: How is a cell phone like a bowl of cereal? List five ways.

219. Complete this sentence ten different ways:

Disappointment is …

220. It was nice.

Turn that sentence into a paragraph that makes us see what was nice and what was nice about it. Do not use the word *nice* at all.

221. Write a very short story where this is the first sentence:

Penelope tweeted her break up letter.

And, the last sentence is:

The basketball game ended in a brawl.

222. Joy is so frustrated with herself. She is terrible at small talk. When she chit-chats with coworkers riding up the elevator at work each morning, she always finds herself complaining about the weather. It doesn't matter what the weather is or who she is talking with. Complaints just seem to fall from her lips.

Help Joy out. Write three short scripts that she can use that do *not* involve complaints and that make her sound edgy and interesting—or even mysterious.

223. Vu's parents don't ask much from him. His only chore is to vacuum the family apartment twice a week. That's all.

Vu hates vacuuming, though. He would rather

Unjournaling © Taylor & Francis

load the dishwasher,
clean the toilets, fold the
laundry—do anything but
vacuum. Write a compelling
speech that Vu can give
to his parents at dinner
tomorrow night to convince
them to reassign his
family chore.

224. Jelly is Jovon's jam. He loves
to make it. He loves to eat
it. He loves to invent new
recipes using it. He loves to
replicate his grammy's jelly
recipes.

Jovon is looking for
investors to fund his
very promising business
venture—Jovon's Jelly Jam.
Write a letter to potential
investors expressing why
they should give him a
million dollars for this
winning idea.

225.
Wordle is a wildly popular
online game based on five-
letter words. Make a list of at
least 25 five-letter words and
then arrange them into
a poem.

226. Chewy loves Chipotle,
cheetahs, and chocolate.
Write a paragraph that
describes more about
Chewy using at least 15 *ch*
words that start with a *tch*
sound. (Think *cheese*, not
chemistry or *Chicago*.)

227. "Don't let me keep you,"
Matilda said for the fifth
time to Zeb, who didn't take
the hint that it was time for
him to go home.

Zeb replied, "Don't
worry. You're not keeping
me. I enjoy being here."

Write the rest of the script of a frustrated but polite Matilda trying to get a clueless Zeb to leave.

228.

Pulverize. Disaster. Obliterate. Vicious.

Use these four words in a description of the party for little Becca's third birthday.

229. While running the help desk at the library, Apollonia has become Twitter famous for declaring her truths on Twitter. This viral fame has meant that she has to outsource some of her writing. Help her out by writing three tweet-sized (280 characters or less) declarations for Apollonia about any of these topics: outer space, the color green, dairy products, classic TV shows, strong female protagonists, or Kendrick Lamar.

230. Igor could hardly wait to get his new special license plates for his car. He paid extra for these plates: *BIM-BB1*. Explain the meaning behind this very special license plate.

231. Daiyu decided to go a whole day telling the absolute truth. After only one hour, no one was speaking to her.

Describe some of Daiyu's conversations in that hour. Who did Daiyu talk to? What did she say? How did people react?

232. "Children should go to school only until they are eight years old," said Camilla. She has five clear reasons, though not everyone would agree with them. What are her reasons?

233. Here are examples of sense words: *reeked* (for smell), *sparkled* (for sight), *itched* (for touch), *peeped* (for hearing), and *sour* (for taste). Choose five different sense words and use them all in a descriptive paragraph about some kind of visit.

234. Write a paragraph that uses as many words as possible that contain the letters Q, Z, and X.

235. Nakai is excited. A film company wants to produce the movie he has written. The only problem? The producers want to change his title. He calls his movie *Fluffy-Muffy and the Menacing Madagascar Hissing Cockroach*.

List five of the reasons the producers gave him for changing the title.

236.
Now list five reasons Nakai gave the producers for keeping the title as *Fluffy-Muffy and the Menacing Madagascar Hissing Cockroach*.

237. Write a synopsis of Nakai's movie, *Fluffy-Muffy and the Menacing Madagascar Hissing Cockroach*. Remember, a synopsis will give the major plot points of the story.

Before you begin, read some examples of a synopsis. For example, you might google "synopsis of *Frozen*" or "synopsis of *The Batman*." Make your synopsis only about a paragraph long.

238.

Mickey and Morgan each wrote an online review of a new video game called *Gorphmallot*. Mickey loved it. Morgan hated it. Each had very specific reasons. What did each write?

239.

Professor Percival speaks in complicated sentences using long, fancy-sounding words. Professor Penelope speaks in short, blunt sentences with few descriptive words. The two sat down to lunch together one day, and this is how the conversation began:

"Although I was not rapacious when we sat down to dine," said Professor Percival, "this aromatic concoction laden with legumes is causing my olfactory receptors to twitch, and I am feeling more ravenous than previously. I am eager to consume what appears might be a gastronomic delight."

"Beef stew," said Professor Penelope. "Yum. I'm hungry. Let's eat."

Continue their conversation as they discuss other foods served, people around them, their work together, or other topics.

240.

List ten things that a person might see on the street. Then write a paragraph that includes all the items but without using the verbs *is* or *are*.

Unjournaling © Taylor & Franci

241.

Stefano hates math story problems. He thinks story problems like this are stupid:

If there are 20 children at a party and five of them are eating vanilla ice cream, five are eating chocolate, and two are eating strawberry, how many children are eating rocky road?

"Why not just look at the ones eating rocky road and *count* them?" he asks. "Or ask something more interesting, like 'How many of the children eating ice cream think that ghosts are real?'"

He decides to vent his frustration by writing the most ridiculous math story problem he can thinking of, including the following items: *wedges of cheese, ladybugs, cousins, backscratchers, centimeters, cacti, and car tires.* His problem is more than 50 words long, and so is his answer. What did he write?

242. Write an unlikely love story between Mr. Unruly Eyebrow Face and Ms. Starla Stompy Stompington. Why these nicknames? How do they meet?

243. Holy heifers! The letter *H* has hexed Hazel. She has a need to use it as much as possible. Write a paragraph about Hazel using at least half of one hundred words containing H.

244. "It was such a giant mistake," said Greta. Write the rest of this story.

245.

One character in a new graphic novel loves coming up with strange and horrible "Would you rather?" questions like these:

Would you rather run into a grizzly bear cub on a mountain trail OR be locked in a room with an angry skunk?

Would you rather have a thousand paper cuts and be dunked in a vat of lemon juice OR have a thousand wood splinters stuck all over your body, including under your finger nails?

Would you rather sit in a traffic jam for three hours while you need to go to the bathroom OR wait in line for three hours to get tickets to hear your favorite group and then find out the couple ahead of you line line bought the last two tickets?

Write five sets of horrible "Would you rather . . .?" choices for the graphic novel.

246. Conway Twitty was an old country music star with an obviously made-up name. His name comes from the names of two towns in Arkansas.

Create an imaginary famous musician using two town names in your state. Write a paragraph describing this star and his or her music.

247.

Headless Mike was an actual chicken who lived without a head for a year and a half. Write a fictional account of this chicken's wild 18-month adventure without a head. (You can use Google to find out more about the true story *after* you write.)

248.

Elias describes himself as a true "grammar cop." He constantly criticizes his twin sister Eliza for using what he calls "nonwords"—words that people use a lot but that are not *quite* and aren't considered "proper" English. Here are some examples:

- accrost (instead of across)
- irregardless (instead of regardless)
- expresso (instead of espresso)
- excetera (instead of etcetera)
- supposably (instead of supposedly)
- prolly (instead of probably)
- ginormous (instead of enormous)
- flustrated (instead of frustrated)
- funner (instead of more fun)

Write a conversation between Elias and Eliza in which Eliza uses nonwords and Elias is not pleased. Use as many nonwords as possible for Eliza.

249. Bonita's boyfriend Blue just broke up with her, and she *is* blue. Write a soliloquy where Bonita bemoans the loss of her beloved beau, using a billion (or at least 30) words that start with B.

250.

Four-year-old Mandisa has just discovered the power of the question "Why?" Take a well-known fairy tale and write 15–20 questions that Mandisa asks about specific details in the story.

sample responses

DOI: 10.4324/9781003278559-3

NOTE: A number of people of varying ages, from 5–83, were the guinea pigs for *Unjournaling*, trying out all the writing prompts and helping us refine the questions. The sample responses that follow are taken from our collaboration with these very patient individuals.

The responses are in no way meant to be models of what *ought* to be done. Because many of the prompts are unusual or not easy to complete, students (and sometimes teachers!) may sometimes find themselves stumped. The samples are included to show how others have approached each item.

Thank you to all the individuals who collaborated with us on the samples: Edward Armstrong, Lisa Blankenship, Mario Markuson DiPrince, Mary Gutting, Pat Howard, Joy Kalamen, Andrew Ketelsen, Braiden Ketelsen, Brodrick Ketelsen, Carter Ketelsen, Amy Madden, Heather Madigan, Susan Malmstadt, Samantha Prust, Patsy Shouse, Shirley Wilsey, Deb Wycoff.

Dawn DiPrince and Cheryl Miller Thurston

1. Dot loved where she grew up, on the farm. She could never see herself as an urban dweller. She loved to be among the flowers, vegetables, cows and horses. Her mother encouraged her to go to school to become a nurse because Dot loved to help people, but Dot couldn't see herself anywhere else but on the farm.

2. *Silly* is dressing to match your poodle.

   Silly is a ten-year-old with an attitude and a pack of Marlboros, thinking he looks so cool that others are looking at him with envy.

   Silly is doing the same thing the same way, over and over again, and then looking surprised to see the same results.

3. My friend **Brea** and I **agree** that it is important to save small creatures from danger when need be. It is not uncommon to **see** us in our living rooms catching a **flea** or a **bee** and taking it outside. Brea even climbed up a **tree** so that **she** could see a little bug she had set **free**. We often **plea** with others to be as kind as **we** are. **Gee**, that would please **me**!

4. My ornery cat Snooker likes to tease and torment my sweet cat Marigold. He swats at her when she walks by and then lunges at her when she growls at him. He hunches down on all fours, does a little wiggle and then leaps up in the air and plops down right on top of her. It looks and sounds like two baby cougars vying for the role of alpha feline.

5. My worst chore is cleaning the little wad of unidentifiable food particles out of the kitchen sink drain. The gunk reminds me of rotting vegetables and old hamburger grease all mixed

together. To get it out, you have to reach in and try to grab it, but it's slimy and it oozes out between your fingers. It smells bad, too—kind of like liver and okra casserole. I wouldn't be at all surprised to see cleaning the sink basket show up on an episode of *Fear Factor* someday.

6. A cowboy in a ten-gallon hat comes blasting through the saloon doors with a look on his face that says he would like to flatten someone. The bartender bravely says, "Howdy. What can I get you?"

"Give me a strong drink," says the cowboy. "I just got fired."

"You must be upset," says the bartender, pouring the drink.

"I'm upset about getting fired, but I'm not upset about not being a cowboy anymore. I never wanted to be a cowboy in the first place."

"Really?"

"No. People take one look at me and think I'm a tough guy. I'm not. Inside I'm really a kind, sensitive guy."

"You could have fooled me," says the bartender, looking at the scar down the cowboy's face and his calloused hands. "What would you like to do instead?"

"What I'd really like to do is become a bartender."

The bartender stares at him in amazement and says, "You're kidding! All I ever wanted to do was be a cowboy!"

The cowboy trades his ten-gallon hat for an apron and starts washing glasses. The bartender walks out with a smile on his face, in search of a horse.

7. In the deep, dark woods, we never know what may be leaping or creeping through the weeds. It's best to keep our hoods on tight as we scoot through the underbrush in our boots. If we hear an owl hoot, we need to heed the warning and speed home quickly, taking care not to fall and make ourselves bleed. However, we should not brood over our fright. Instead, we should sit by a brook and feed ourselves some loopy noodles, for soon we will be back in the city, listening to motor scooters and horns tooting.

8. • "When you-know-what freezes over," said Jim's mother after he asked her when he could adopt a boa constrictor.
   • When the measure came up for a vote, the representative said, "Nay."
   • "Over my dead body!" yelled Samantha, after Edward asked for his ring back.
   • "Entry forbidden to anyone under 21," said the sign on the club door, making it apparent to the sixteen-year-olds that they weren't going to be partying there.
   • When Max asked his dad if he could borrow his BMW for prom night, the answer was a simple, "Dream on, sonny."
   • After a tree slammed through a window and smashed her television, Teresa's insurance claim came back stamped "Denied."
   • When David asked his boss if he would get a raise this year, she said, "Negative."
   • Shelby asked if she could get an extension on the assignment, but her teacher said it was "so unlikely as to be impossible."

- When the candidate asked if I would vote for him, I politely said, "I believe I'd rather not."
- Lily asked Benjamin out on a date, but he replied, cruelly, "Not if you were the last girl on earth."

9. Dear Mr. Sharp:

    Thank you for the opportunity to manage Widget World. I have enjoyed this position for over three years and would like to point out some of the ways I have helped the company.

    Last month, I suggested extra security lights and cameras added to the parking lot. Customers and employees commented that they feel safer and are very thankful for the concern we showed for their safety.

    In an attempt to boost sales, I initiated the redesign of our logo to make it clearer what Widget World actually sells. Since the updated logo has been in use, our brand recognition has improved and more customers than ever before have visited the Widget World store, both in person and online, resulting in a 20% increase in business in just the last three months.

    I welcome the opportunity to talk with you in person about ways I have helped Widget World and can continue to help it in the future. I hope you will agree that a raise for me is in order.

    Sincerely,
    Holly Holder

10. S: Sick
    E: elephants
    N: never
    T: try
    E: energetic,
    N: nimble
    C: cartwheels,
    E: ever.

11. The tiny gymnast **bounced** up onto the balance beam and performed an incredible routine while the spectators **roared** their approval. When her score was posted, she **collapsed** into the arms of her coach, who gave her a big bear hug. Then she **spied** her mom and dad creating quite a ruckus on the sideline and she **giggled** uncontrollably. She **struggled** to regain her composure when she saw the TV cameras aimed at her, but she didn't succeed.

12. As the teacher droned on about statistics and pie charts, Ernie's eyes glazed over and his head started to droop. His teacher spoke sharply, and Ernie blinked his eyes, shook his head and took a deep breath. How he wished he were in English class where he could be doing goofy but interesting writing assignments. He started counting the tiles in the floor, just so he wouldn't fall asleep.

13. Melanie finally exercised intensely following Saturday's basketball tournament.

14. Living in a duplex with thin walls, Yasmin was understandably apprehensive when a new neighbor moved in. Her fears were realized when, just days later, her ears were assaulted with the sounds of a tortured cat scraping her claws down a chalkboard. The neighbor played the violin, about on the level of a deaf monkey. After several days of agony, Yasmin approached the neighbor but barely opened her mouth before she was lambasted with a twenty-minute diatribe on civil rights, noise ordinances, and personal freedom. She slunk back home, pondered her situation, and purchased a set of bagpipes. The neighbor moved out a week later.

15. This striped version of our classic crew neck sweater is sure to spice up your winter wardrobe with bands of burned cinnamon mixed with citrus-fire twist. And as if that weren't enough—a subtle lavender musk takes its turn with a tailored tan to make this sweater a must-have.

16. • Opera? Seriously? Have you ever met me, Grandpa? I mean, really, do you want to torture me or what?
    • If I play one more game of "Go Fish," I will have to go to bed with a headache. You don't want me to be sick, do you? Wouldn't that be awful? Then I couldn't play *anything* with you.
    • After having spent the entire day making myself look fabulous with a pedicure, manicure and getting my hair done, I have no desire to douse myself in eau de fish and the accompanying but equally earthy *eau de sweat*. I will be relaxing and resting, and I hope the fish do likewise.

17. The constant yap-yap-yapping of the peek-a-poo puppy on the porch next door was making Alfred wish with all his heart that he did not work from a home office.

18. Blueberries Raining Over the Ocean
    Cherries Exploding in a Fire
    Lemon, Banana, Squash Smoothie

19. • Like looking for a sugar crystal in a sack of flour.
    • Like looking for an eyelash in the ocean.
    • Like trying to find a marshmallow dropped in a snow drift.
    • Like hunting for a blonde hair in a field of wheat.
    • Like trying to find a flea in a barrel of pepper.

20. Talia jumped rope. So did Lina.
    Wyatt came over. Wyatt is four. He jumped, too.
    Talia jumped faster. So did Lina.
    Wyatt yelled, "Slower!"
    Talia ignored him.
    Lina laughed.
    Wyatt ran away.
    Talia laughed. "Works every time."
    Lina smiled. "Like a charm."

· *Unjournaling* © Taylor & Franci

21. There was confusion and chaos Tuesday morning in the Blueberry East subdivision. Eyewitnesses claim that a block-wide area was flooded with gallons of a pink substance said to be liquid bubblegum.

    According to eyewitnesses, Al Conway, who resides at 427 East Magnolia, brought home a big barrel labeled "Contents Under Pressure" over the long holiday weekend. When neighbors asked him what it was, Conway said, "My kids chew bubblegum like it's going out of style. I can't get them to stop because my wife does the same thing. So, I've decided to make my own bubblegum."

    A close friend of the Conway family, John Gibbons, helped Conway pick up a washing machine just days before the incident. According to Gibbons, Conway bought the new Galaxy 773-X front-loading washing machine and said, "We have special plans for this Galaxy!"

    Although police have not been able to interview Conway yet, due to his hospitalization for an undisclosed injury, they speculate that he used the Galaxy 773-X to make the bubblegum but bit off a bit more than he could chew. Neighbors called police when they noticed the pink gooey substance oozing from all the doors and windows of the modest ranch home.

22. Angela rolled her eyes. Jerome spit out the soda he was drinking. Seven-year-old Jake laughed loudly and snorted a lot while his mother shook her head back and forth. Jake's friend Sam actually fell on the floor and rolled around, holding his stomach.

23.   Go, Sharks, go!
        You're not slow!
        We think you're great!
        So activate!

24. • Never count your doggie treats before they're thrown.
    • When you want something, put your head on your owner's leg and look pathetic.
    • Greet each day with a stretch, a wiggle, and a smile.
    • Lick children's faces to show that you like them. Don't be offended if they scream.

25. • Doing nothing automatically makes everyone else seem more productive, thus boosting their self-esteem.
    • Doing nothing gives you time to think. A lot.
    • Doing nothing helps you remember what's important in life.
    • Doing nothing gives your body a break.
    • Doing nothing may annoy others, thus giving you a way to get back at people who have annoyed you.

26. Her fingers were long and thin, capped by black nail polish. A tattoo of a snake wrapped around her thumb and up her wrist. On her left hand was a ring with a large green stone, etched with a drawing of a dragon breathing fire.

27. When **Carl** the **carpenter** got a job **caring** for the **carousel** at the **carnival,** he was so happy that he did a **cartwheel.** On the morning of his first day on the job, he ate a hearty breakfast filled with **carbohydrates** because his boss had told him that his first task would be to repair a couple of statues on the ride, namely the **caribou** and the **cardinal.** After fixing the statues, he went by the **caramel** corn stand and got a treat. Then he **carried** a **carafe** of water to the **caricature** artist because she looked parched. She was grateful and in turn gave him a **carnation** to wear on his shirt lapel. (Score: $140)

28. Lucky Charms Marshmallow Cluster Potato Chips
Thanksgiving Dinner Potato Chips
Caesar Salad with Anchovy Dressing Potato Chips
Barbacoa Street Tacos with Pineapple Salsa Potato Chips
Beef Ramen Potato Chips

    What could be tastier than combining the sweet taste of Lucky Charms Marshmallow Clusters with the salty spiciness of potato chips? Your mouth will turn into a smile when you bite into one of these delicious chips, and you certainly won't be able to stop with just one. Stock up now because you are going to *love* Lucky Charms Marshmallow Cluster Potato Chips!

29. Captain Mystic was a soldier in Vietnam who was redeployed in 1970 to a secret lab where spy agents were trying to encode messages into disco albums to infiltrate the youth dance scene. While working in this top secret lab, he was exposed to stardust from outer space and gained superpowers including superhuman yet graceful strength, superhuman flexibility, and supersonic hearing skills. Anonymous officials saw this mishap as an opportunity for him to go undercover in the disco world. His new skills made him king of the dance floor, with the new name Captain Mystic, winning acclaim in dance competitions while also giving him superhuman traits to fight against evil everywhere. During a security shut down, Captain Mystic was able to escape from the anonymous officials and live his life on his own terms. While he is older now with gray hair and bad eyesight, he still has superhuman grace, strength, flexibility, and hearing. He loves to tell stories of dancing during the high disco days, and he now uses his superpowers to protect young people and their desire to dance and listen to funky beats from meddling anonymous officials.

30. Zookeeper Yolanda x-rays whales vigorously under the strict regimen quoted. Pandas often need more love. Kangaroos jump into hydrangeas. Giraffes find everything delicious: corn, beans, and apricots.

31. My mom's mutt Rusty won't run. Rusty trots or stops. Soon, my mom must tow Rusty.

32. Dad: Dearest son, the dishes require cleaning, like a human needs oxygen. I fear they will become our foe, if we do not cleanse them. The unclean vessels will prevent further use of the sink and all of its purposes.

    Mom: Do the dishes!

33. As I entered the kitchen, I was surprised to see smoke pouring from my dishwasher. Alarmed at the possibility of a fire burning out of control, I quickly put on some gloves and filled a bucket with water. Then I opened the dishwasher door and fanned the smoke away.

    To my dismay, the smoke kept coming, so I poured on the water. Finally, the smoke stopped. Then, to my shock, a genie popped out of the dishwasher. I was so startled that I fell backwards and dropped the bucket. The genie looked mad.

    "Why'd you go and do that?" said the genie.

    "Uh, what?!"

    "Why'd you dump that water on me?"

    "I'm sorry, I guess...I was just kind of worried about the possibility of my house burning down," I mumbled.

    "Well, I think you were being a bit paranoid. However, now that I'm standing here, I might as well give you your three wishes."

    "Really? I get three wishes? Great! My first wish is that you never spit smoke from your bottle in my dishwasher again."

    The genie sighed. "Granted."

    "Now for my other wishes..." I smiled. "Why don't you just dry off? These are going to take me a little time..."

34. Mold Spice: Ripped Muscle Shirt Scent.
    Same Bottle, Worse Product!
    Mold Spice can be used for everything from shampoo and conditioner to cleaning your drain of grease. It contains sulfates, which may damage hair and skin. It also contains microbeads that pollute the ocean and kill fish. It smells like a middle school hallway. It appeals to men who are proud to call themselves macho. Hair becomes greasy and somehow also crispy when it is used. A gasoline alternative!

35. • Go on a 50 mile bike ride to her Auntie Liz's and back.
    • Go whitewater rafting with the youth group at school.
    • Take the Victor's burrito challenge at Roja's restaurant.
    • Overcome fear of spiders by adopting a pet tarantula.
    • Volunteer to feed the giraffes at the local zoo.

36. It's like your nose fills up with a thick, clay-like substance and someone pounds it in, hard, and you can't escape, no matter how hard you sneeze or blow your nose. It stays stuffed up there in your nose, and you can't get away from it, no matter what you do, despite how much it pains you and makes your eyes water and your stomach churn.

37. "Right after my 25th win on *Jeopardy*."
    "When television is banned from the planet."
    "As soon as aliens land on Earth in broad daylight."
    "When my dad stops rooting for the Cubs."
    "When I win a lifetime supply of tennis shoes from Nike."
    "When celebrities in America make minimum wage."

"When teachers in America make six-figure incomes."

"When squirrels go waterskiing…no, wait—they have. When lizards go waterskiing."

38. Yankee Doodle was starving the day he came riding to town. After all, there were no fast food joints back then. He hadn't eaten for days and, as a result, was quite delirious. He was dreaming of his favorite dish, macaroni and cheese, drooling over the thought of gooey orange sauce covering tender noodles, when an admiring lady at the side of the road handed him a feather to adorn his hat. He had enough sense to accept the feather and put it in his cap, but when he tried to say "Thank you," all that came out was "macaroni." Before he could correct himself and explain his situation, the woman shook her head and backed off. She told everyone she knew about the strange guy who called a feather "macaroni."

    And the woman really did know *everyone*.

39.   Shannon crumpled under the pressure of the final exam in her underwater basket-weaving class.

    Harry showed up two days late to the job interview at Disneyland, wearing a crumpled tie.

    The chihuahuas crumpled to the floor after a long day of barking at every single vehicle that passed their Winnebago.

40. Lisa lost her power of speech whenever Chris was around. As she caught sight of him entering the gym with some other boys, she froze and just stared. Her friend Lisa dropped her cupcake. The boys backed off, warily, and turned around, rolling their eyes. The girls, however, cautiously approached him, smiling and blushing—that is, except for Lisa, who hadn't managed to move yet.

41. When the child ran behind the bush to get her ball, she was startled by a strange creature perched on top of the ball, staring at her. It glowed pink and had a large, black, tree-like appendage sprouting from its head. When the little girl crouched down to get a better look at the creature, it jumped into her hand.

    "Oh, do you want to be friends?" asked the little girl. The creature answered by curling up in a ball and falling asleep. At least she thought that's what it was doing. She wasn't sure with pink extraterrestrials.

    "I'm going to call you Kinkle," she said. She took Kinkle inside and made a little bed for it in her dresser drawer.

    The next day, the little girl awoke to her parents yelling. When she opened her eyes, there were giant black tree branches crisscrossing her room. Some of the branches had ripped through the walls of her bedroom. Birds sat on the branches, singing their songs as if nothing were amiss. There, on one of the branches, sat Kinkle.

42. (to the tune of "All I Have to Do Is Dream" by the Everly Brothers)

    I hate them so much, I could cry.
    I hate them so, and that is why
    Whenever I see peas, all that I can do is

screa-ea-ea-ea-eam, scream, scream, scream.

When I see peas, I want to gag.
When they appear, it's such a drag.
Whenever I see peas, all I want to do is
Screa-ea-ea-ea-eam.

I hate them a bunch.
Don't want them for lunch,
Or anytime, night or day.
Only trouble is, gee whiz,
I'm screaming my life away.

I hate them so much, I could cry.
I hate them so, and that is why,
Whenever I see peas, all I want to do is
Srea-ea-ea-ea-eam, scream, scream, scream.
(Fade) Screa-ea-ea-ea-eam, scream scream scream.

43. My mom bought an old plum colored car and gave it to me on my 16th birthday. The engine doesn't sound too good, but the body is in good shape, smooth as an eggshell, and the seat covers are as soft as peach fuzz. It runs okay, but it has an old car smell that reminds me of moldy bread. I sure hope it doesn't turn out to be a lemon.

44. I'm all alone in the house late at night, and I hear loud wailing sounds coming up the dimly lit basement stairs, punctuated by heavy footsteps.

45. Make sure your Tonka wheels are always firmly on the ground, just like a real truck.

The potty is specially reserved just for you to put your #1 and #2 in. Mommy's shoes go on a special shoe rack in the closet.

Let's draw your pretty elephants on this nice paper to keep in your special picture book forever, instead of on the walls where they'll get painted over if we move someday.

46. I am one true, loyal friend—totally, honestly, genuinely.

47. Chairs have four legs because...
...it makes them harder to knock over.
...they are more symmetrical than they would be with three legs.
...because any more legs would just be in the way.
...because somebody a long time ago invented the four-legged chair and nobody's come up with anything better.
...because with four legs, they match tables, which also have four legs.
...because the union of chair leg manufacturers is very strong and won't let companies decrease the number of legs on chairs because the union members would have less work.
...because nine or ten legs would just look silly.
...because it's tradition, and no one wants to go against tradition.

48. King Kong screamed at the scurrying pedestrians. He lunged at the barking dogs as he swung at the shrieking cats. He pounded his fists on his chest and hurled hot dog vendors to the pier. He blew cars and buses out of his path. He kicked tall buildings until they fell to the ground.

49. For the most contemporary designs in light blocking and privacy blinds, choose Zebra Wink. When the Zebra Winks, you're in the dark.

50.   "Stop your bellyaching and get your chores done," Mom said sternly.

     "I'm too tired," Joey whined. "Do I have to?"

     "Absolutely," Mom replied. "If you had done your chores instead of complaining, you'd be done now."

     "I know, I know," Joey moaned. "I never do anything right. All you ever do is criticize me."

     "Poor baby," Mom said. "You suffer so."

     Joey looked up hopefully.

     Mom folded her arms and gave him a look. "Yes, my heart is breaking for you, but I'll have to cry later…after you do your chores. Now, move!"

51. Alison Krauss is undoubtedly the most unbelievably incredible fiddle playin' bluegrass singer ever to cross the Mason-Dixon line. She sings the saddest, most heartbreaking, tear-jerking love songs ever heard since the beginning of time. When she tunes up and starts singing those sad tunes in that whispery velvet voice of hers, you can practically hear the collective heartbreak of the entire human race and feel the infinite flood of billions and billions of tears as if the stars were falling down from the heavens.

52. • Why can't I be the only one who's gluten-free this week?
    • I love my smoothies, but why does the blender have to be SO noisy this early in the morning?
    • Why does my mom have to pack me these healthy lunches? Can't I even get a bag of chips in here?
    • It is so unfair that I have to pay for my own gas in my car. I mean, I'm doing them a favor by driving myself everywhere.
    • Why does this credit card have a limit? Who does that?

53. Anne's hair looks like it grows right out of her brain, with masses of auburn frizz flying every which way at once, shooting bolts of lightning when she gets another good idea. As soon as she opens the door, I can see what she's been up to. There's a pencil behind one ear, a glob of oatmeal behind the other one, and glitter everywhere.

My other best friend has long, straight black hair all the way down to her chair when she sits. It all stays exactly in the right place all the time. Well, almost all the time. Once in a while her bangs have other ideas. They stick straight up like they want to fly away. And sometimes a piece of long hair falls over her shoulder and she twirls it under her nose like a mustache!

54. The grackelty hoovimelt with a creachemous blorsal plurdled and blurdled to the storny roopst where the woppetty plorkel zoozened.

55. fit as a fiddle, hit the hay, saved by the bell, rustle up some grub, down for the count, work like a dog, tougher than shoe leather, out like a light, stubborn as a mule, eat like a horse

    My Uncle Buff is a lumberjack. He works like a dog cutting, lifting and hauling logs. All that work makes him as fit as a fiddle. After working hard all day, he sometimes collapses with exhaustion and seems like he's down for the count. Fortunately, he's usually saved by the bell—the dinner bell, that is. Then it's time to rustle up some grub. Uncle Buff eats like a horse and it doesn't matter if his steak is as tough as shoe leather. He just keeps chewing. He won't give up until he gets it all down—he's as stubborn as a mule. By the time he's through with his dinner and all that chewing, he's ready to watch a little TV and then hit the hay. He's so worn out, he's out like a light in five minutes.

56. My Uncle Buff is a lumberjack. He works like a machine, cutting, lifting and hauling logs. All that work makes him as fit as any Olympian. Still, after working hard all day, he sometimes collapses with exhaustion and looks so dead that his wife often checks to make sure he is breathing. Fortunately, hunger pangs usually bring him back to the world of the living, and he goes in search of food. Uncle Buff eats like the champion of an extreme eating challenge, and it doesn't matter what he eats, even if it's steak that is as tough as the skin of a rhinoceros. He just keeps chewing. He won't give up until he gets it all down—he's as stubborn as a toddler throwing a fit in the grocery store because he can't have a packet of Fudgy Sugar Bombs. By the time Uncle Buff is through with his dinner, he's ready to watch a little TV and then say hello to his mattress. He's always so worn out that in five minutes he's out like a boxer who's been KO'd.

57. Tattoos are designs people put permanently on their bodies. They don't have a practical use, but people like them to show off something they think is cool or believe in. They go to a tattoo artist who uses a needle with ink to draw it on the skin. People usually choose designs that mean something to them, like maybe the name a boyfriend or girlfriend or just a picture they think is cool. The problem is that the person may break up with the boyfriend or girlfriend and still have their name right where they have to see it every day. And what if it is a bad breakup? They probably suffer even more. People sometimes pay a lot of money to get a tattoo taken off when they don't like it any more. That hurts, too. It may seem like a weird custom, but it is very popular.

58. Dear Kelly,

    As you know, I have expressed feelings of love for you and would like to ask you to consider joining our mutual goals and assets in a marital union. If you would like to accept this offer, we can discuss all the pertinent details at a scheduled appointment time that is agreeable to both of us. If your response is favorable, please contact me as soon as possible, as I would like to begin planning our future together.

    Faithfully yours,
    Pax

59.　　　If we can send a man to the moon, surely we can figure out how to send a woman to the White House.

　　　If we can send a man to the moon, surely we can find a way to make cars run on water or some other inexpensive substance, so that we aren't dependent on the Middle East for oil.

　　　If we can send a man to the moon, surely we can figure out a way to make health insurance affordable for everyone in the country.

　　　If we can send a man to the moon, surely we can find a way to make cell phones shut off automatically in public gatherings.

　　　If we can send a man to the moon, surely we can figure out a way to make television pay for itself without commercials.

60. Cats are the best thing for eliminating rats. They also make mice go away. These kitties can sometimes cause you to sneeze. They like to play with catnip-filled mice every day.

61. "Enjoy the view of those *spacious skies and amber waves of grain!*" my mom yelled as I was walking to the bus for summer camp. I was so embarrassed. A boy with a safety pin through his ear lobe laughed at me, and a girl with black fingernails and green hair rolled her eyes. As I walked by them I muttered under my breath, *"I've a feeling we're not in Kansas anymore."*

62. These days the autumn breeze from up in the trees causes everyone to sneeze. I also sneeze and wheeze when I eat cheese or Wheaties. I guess I'm allergic to these. My dog is allergic to fleas and bees. He's better off when he's catching some Z's. My mom agrees that we should not tease those who sneeze. We'll all feel better after there is a freeze.

63. Have you ever noticed how car dealers like to lure customers in to their big sales? They advertise great deals in order to reel the buyers in and give them the sales pitch. Once they hook the customer into thinking they have just the right car, they pull the old bait-and-switch routine. The advertised deal is gone, but they have this other car, much nicer, with fancy fins and a really cool paint job. It costs a little more, but with the customer's net income, affording it is no problem. Before you know it, the car dealer has tipped the scales for the buyer and he drives away in a new car, thinking this time he's caught the big one. Sounds like a fish story to me.

64. Yesterday morning, I was hanging out as usual on the back bumper of the family car. It had been a cold night, so I was all frosted over. Finally, my owner came out to go to work, coffee in hand and eyes still at half-mast. She backed out of the drive a little too fast, whacking me on the curb. At least I knew I was awake then. She proceeded to run a stop sign in her rush to get to work on time and barely missed hitting another car. Lucky for her, no one could get my number—I was still covered in frost.

65. Lou doesn't have a clue about how to woo. He invited Pru to the zoo, but then he got the flu, turned an awful hue, and had to spend the day in the loo. When he got better, he decided to try anew. He bought some glue and made a flirty card for Pru, but he grew nervous and didn't go through with it. I think in a few more days, Lou will get his courage up and try something new. Perhaps he will figure out that Pru is due a slew of roses.

66. Dear Mr. & Mrs. Dunkle,

As I'm sure you know, Andrew is certainly a very active little boy. We are having a bit of a challenge in getting him to focus his energy on learning. For example, he's having a hard time understanding that focusing his energy on learning doesn't mean ripping up the textbooks or kicking over desks. I'm sure, with your help, we will get over this hump in his educational journey.

Andrew also has quite an advanced vocabulary. Most six-year-olds don't have words like "muddle-headed nincompoop" trip off their tongues, and he needs a bit of help in learning which of his many words are appropriate for the classroom. Perhaps we can start with helping him learn that my name is Miss Shackleford, and not Miss Dimwitted Dunderhead. There are also a few less-than-refined words he needs to learn to keep reserved for some very private part of his brain.

At lunchtime, it's clear that Andrew loves food, not just for eating, but for manipulating, so I recommend an art class as a creative outlet. Mashed potatoes on indoor/outdoor carpet is not, in my opinion, the proper medium for his talents.

Finally, Andrew needs to learn to curb his impulse to whack something whenever he hears the word "No." He needs to learn that fellow students are not for pounding with his Nikes. He needs to learn that paste is not for eating, and chalk is not for stomping on, and paper is not for wadding up and throwing.

I look forward to working with you to help solve our special challenges with Andrew and help us all have a good year for your highly energetic little boy.

Sincerely,
Miss Shackleford

67. Penelope preened her pretty ponytail while posing with purple parrots for a picture to put on her personal postcards. She purchased pink paper to print her picture postcards on. The printing press produced plenty of practically perfect postcards for Penelope. Penelope then parked her parents' Pontiac at the post office and put her postcards in the postal box. Afterward, she picked up a pepperoni personal pan pizza and proceeded to a party. She's probably plumb pooped by now.

68. Winter is my favorite season.
When winter sets in, I come alive
Weekends with skiing, ice skating, snowboarding
Wet clothes and snowball fights
Wiping out on a run
Wishing for snow
Wonderful

69. The black and white panda seems quiet today. The panda chews sugar canes. The panda loves trees. The panda hates cages. The panda looks happy.

70. photograph, physician, phone, phase, phantom, pharmacy, Phoenix, philosopher, phobia, photocopy

When I answered the phone, my aunt said, "Hello! I just got back from my physician, who said I have a computer phobia." I suggested she try drinking some chamomile tea to calm herself down, but she didn't have any. Since she is also afraid of going to the store by herself, I said I would get some for her. While at the grocery store, I decided to pick up my prescription from the pharmacy. As I was waiting, I ran into a philosopher from Phoenix. He claims that making photocopies of photographs is a way to make yourself smarter.

Just when I thought my day couldn't get any stranger, the school principal called and told me that she was having a problem with my brother. He refuses to go to physical education class. Apparently, he's going through a phase where he thinks phantoms are real, and believes there are ghosts in the boys' locker room.

71. Professor Bumbletoes and his team of student sleuths are at it again with *Slithering Secrets*, the much anticipated sequel to *Roaring Riddles*. A relaxing vacation near the swamps of Florida turns treacherous as the gang realizes that people around town are disappearing, starting with the the fortune teller in the town square. Will they discover the secret of the swamp before it swallows up anyone else? Join brave Blair, clever Cory, rambunctious Riley, and everyone's favorite Professor Bumbletoes as they wriggle through more tight spots.

72. Anchorage, Alaska, is home to the legendary astronaut, Jake Phillips. Mr. Phillips was a student of astronomy who wrote five books on the subject. In actuality, he likes to attribute his passion for space to his parents, who are from Australia. It should be no surprise that Mr. Phillips himself will be the authority at the next Astronaut Recruitment Fair. Every day during the event, Mr. Phillips and his assistant will lead audiences in an amazingly adept lecture that is sure to inspire all promising young astronauts to pursue a career in space.

73.   "The grass smells red." John looked confused as he pulled in another deep breath. Everybody around John ignored his statement. People were busy painting pumpkins and anxiously waiting for the corn maze to open. John decided to say it again, louder. "The grass smells red!"

"Finally, a gentleman to his left answered him. "The grass is not dead."

"I didn't say the grass was 'dead.' I said the grass smells 'red,'" said John.

"That doesn't even make sense," replied the gentleman.

"Yes, it does. The grass smells red, meaning the grass smells like blood."

"You're a strange, strange man," the gentleman said as he backed away and alerted the police on his cell phone.

74. • Baffled: This is a simple three shelf bookcase from Ikea, and yet the directions have me *baffled*.
    • Bewildered: Tristan looked up and down the trail and recognized nothing, totally *bewildered* by his surroundings.
    • Stumped: Annabelle was certain that she had the solution to the problem, but she was *stumped* by the professor's description of the first step to solve the differential equation.

- Stupefied: Although this is a third grade math problem, the terminology around unions and intersections has me *stupefied*.
- Dumbfounded: How you, a brilliant person, can support such a wild conspiracy theory leaves me *dumbfounded*.

75. Ugly words: hate, puke, surgery, sick, phlegm, scaly, scab, slimy, putrid, terrible.

I hate phlegm. When I am sick with a cough I wish I could have surgery to remove the slimy phlegm so I don't feel like puking. I'd rather be in a skateboard crash than cough up phlegm. Of course, getting in a crash means dealing with scaly scabs. And if you're in a really bad accident, you can break your leg or arm or something, and then you will have to have a cast. Then, when the cast comes off, you will have to deal with the putrid smell—a terrible thing.

76.   "How are you doing?" asked Ted.
"You know I'm moving, right?" replied Sandra.
"What? Moving?"
"Didn't Amber tell you?"
"Was she supposed to?"
"Don't you two have study hall together?"
"She was supposed to tell me in study hall?"
"Wasn't she in study hall yesterday?"
"Didn't she leave early for a basketball trip yesterday?"
"So she didn't tell you because she was gone?"

77.   "Yipes!" said the zebra. "I've lost my stripes."
"Cripes! What's the hype?" said the horse.
"I said I've lost my stripes," said the zebra. "Now I'm a regular old horse like you."
"That's a stupid gripe," said the horse.
"Shut your windpipe!" said the zebra.
"Well, I may be a regular old horse—maybe even a stereotype, but I would rather think of myself as an archetype, if you don't mind."
"You can go play the bagpipes for all I care," said the zebra.
"Well, aren't you a guttersnipe!" said the horse. "Maybe if you had my blood type you wouldn't be so mean."
"I'm sorry," said the zebra. "I'm just so upset! My imagination is ripe with the **awful** scenarios of what it will be like to live without stripes."
"Maybe you can type a letter to the stripes people asking for the prototype for stripes. In the meantime you can wear a striped shirt and some striped tights so no one will notice you've lost them."
"Thanks, Horse. I'm sorry I took a swipe at you for being a horse. I guess I'm really attached to my stripes," said the zebra, crying.
"Wipe your tears," said the horse. "Here's a Handi Wipe."
"Thanks," said the zebra. "I haven't met a horse this nice since the days of tintype."

78. I love the part of the year from June through July. I love hot weather and cold watermelon. You can jump in a cool pool, eat ice cream, wear your favorite tee, barbeque, stay up late, hang out all the time with your BFF, loiter at the park. And, I love no homework, no uniform, little obligation, and I don't have to wake up early in the morning. I want the whole year to be exactly like June and July.

79. Anne's eyes grew wide when her mom set her birthday cake on the tray in front of her. She giggled as her hands squished through the icing. With her fingers covered in icing and cake, she shoved them into her mouth and giggled some more. The icing smeared across her face like clown makeup, and her hands wore gloves of cake. It would take a long bath to get the birthday cake off the toddler.

80. Bernard heard the buzz of the city all around him as he sloshed down the street. Passing cars beeped at each other in their hurried way. Bernard's boots went splat on the wet cement. He heard the loud clang of bells as he passed a church. When he reached his friend's house, he pressed the doorbell. Ding-dong! The door creaked opened and Stanley invited him in. Bernard loved the tick-tock of the cuckoo clock hanging in Stanley's front hallway. As Bernard and Stanley sat down in the living room, Stanley's cat Pickles began scratching the sofa. "No!" said Stanley. The cat hissed, then came over and purred, rubbing against Stanley's leg.

81. Mary had a little fish,
     Little fish, little fish.
     Mary had a little fish.
     She got it in Hong Kong.

     And everywhere that Mary went,
     Mary went, Mary went,
     Everywhere that Mary went
     She brought her fish along.

     She wrote her fish some pretty prose,
     Pretty prose, pretty prose.
     She wrote her fish some pretty prose.
     She was a little strange.

     She dressed it up in fancy clothes,
     Fancy clothes, fancy clothes.
     She dressed it up in fancy clothes.
     Some say she was deranged.

     She always brought her fish to work,
     Fish to work, fish to work.
     She always brought her fish to work
     And set it on her chair.

     Her fellow workers laughed at her,
     Laughed at her, laughed at her.

Her fellow workers laughed at her,
But Mary didn't care.

Mary had the last guffaw,
Last guffaw, last guffaw.
Mary had the last guffaw
When she received a raise.

Why did Mary's boss do this?
Boss do this? Boss do this?
Why did Mary's boss do this?
The others were amazed.

82. My fairy godmother would look like my own mother, with black hair, blue eyes, cute dimples, and a kind smile. The reason my fairy godmother would look like my own mother is because my mom lives in another state and I don't get to see her more than a few times a year. I would want my fairy godmother to look like my mom so I wouldn't miss her so much. My fairy godmother would offer me hugs and advice. She would make special dinners for me every once in a while, like the baked macaroni and cheese topped with tomatoes that my mom makes for me when I'm visiting. My fairy godmother would help me by making me feel better when I'm down. My fairy godmother would be a very cheerful and bubbly person who would remind me that every cloud has a silver lining.

83. I look out my apartment window and see sun filtering through trees and down onto cars, making them shine. I see Mrs. Johnson leaning out her window, shaking a blue and yellow quilt. Her husband, Theodore, exits their brownstone, holding their dog Kipper on a leash.

84. Frank is as exciting as a bowl of instant mashed potatoes.
Celeste has fingers as long as celery stalks.
Angie's eyes are as big as Aunt Reggiano's special Sunday Italian meatballs.
Keith is as weak as a wet noodle in the rain.
Sarah's hair is as dark as burned cookies.
Andy is as energetic as corn kernels popping in a giant popcorn popper at a movie theater.
Arianne is as temperamental as my special cheese souffle—sometimes high,
    sometimes low, sometimes just right.
Emily is as warm and friendly as freshly baked bread sitting on a sunny window sill.
Justin is as sweet as a just-picked pineapple.
Rory looked as pale as the undercooked sugar cookies she was pulling out of the oven.

85. As Antonio opened the door, he gasped to see…
…his family and friends gathered around a birthday cake with lit candles, singing
    "Happy Birthday."
…his new puppy relieving itself on his wife's favorite pair of designer shoes.
…a masked intruder leaving a trail of blood as he fled through the kitchen window.

86. Jack liked a lake. He did feel a gale. He hiked back.

87. The tortilla tasted like old wet cardboard left out in an alley for a week.

88. Dwight and Dwayne are a couple of dweebs who used to dwell in computer research center. They lived there, never even going home at night because they loved sitting at a computer all day. One day they noticed that their assignments were dwindling, and soon they were fired. Uncertain what to do, they drove off and found a cabin in the woods. They decided to live there. Reaching out, they adopted a dweedle bug as a pet, and they named him Dwarple.

89. It's the night of the eighth grade formal dance, and Austin's mom has volunteered to drive Austin and his best friend and their girlfriends to the dance. The boys are looking very grown up and very uncomfortable in their ties and sport jackets. The girls look lovely and shy in their fancy outfits.

    All is going well when mom bursts into a raucous rendition of "Bad Boys." She's giving it all the body language she's got, bopping in time to the music, trying to look cool as she's belting out her song, a little off key. The girls roll their eyes. Austin's best friend slides his eyes over to Austin with a "Can you believe this?" look. Austin just turns beet red and sinks low in the back seat, hoping that no one he knows passes them and that she ends her song before they pull up at the school.

90. Sneaking up behind a Clydesdale horse and giving it a slap on the behind is a bad idea.
    Putting on mascara while driving through rush hour traffic is a bad idea.
    Using a hubcap as an umbrella in a lightning storm is a bad idea.
    Entrusting your toddler to put away your fine china is a bad idea.
    Giving your bank account number and password to a telemarketer selling raffle tickets
        for weekend getaways is a bad idea.
    Asking your parents for an allowance right after you have flunked three subjects and
        wrecked your dad's vintage Corvette is a bad idea.
    Carrying a tall stack of heavy boxes down an icy, slippery fire escape is a bad idea.
    Approaching a grizzly bear with cubs to get a good photograph is a bad idea.
    Letting your baby brother ride piggyback while you're downhill skiing is a bad idea.
    Using a fork to get toast out of the toaster without unplugging it first is a bad idea.

91. What is the opposite of **yes**? No.
    What is the opposite of **no?** Yes.
    What is the opposite of **certainly?** Maybe.
    Can you tell me the answer? What is the question?

92. Miss Klinkfelder watched as the middle-school students in her cooking class removed their cakes from the ovens. To her dismay, all of the cakes were flat.
    "Now, class, you apparently didn't follow the instructions and left an important step out. Did you add flour?"
    The class replied in unison, "Yes."
    "Did you add eggs?"
    "Yes."

"Did you add milk?"

"Yes."

"Did you add baking powder?"

The class didn't answer. One student raised her hand. "Adding baking powder wasn't on your instruction sheet, Miss Klinkfelder."

"Don't be ridiculous," she said. "I wouldn't forget one of the most important ingredients!"

The student walked up and handed the instruction sheet to Miss Klinkfelder.

Miss Klinkfelder read the sheet. She blushed. "Oops," muttered Miss Klinkfelder.

93. After Fatima had opened all of her birthday presents, her parents announced they had one last special present to give her. Her mother went into the other room, came back with a large box wrapped in colorful paper, and then proudly handed it to Fatima. Fatima frowned. This special present was way too small to be a car. Still, perhaps there were keys inside...

Slowly she opened the present. Inside was a brand new laptop computer. As her parents smiled happily, Fatima looked up and started crying. "It's only a laptop computer," she sobbed. "You never get me what I want!" She stomped upstairs to her room and slammed the door.

94. The phrase "You're pulling my leg" arose from an incident that also spawned a whole body of folklore about the Loch Ness monster. It all started when young Sean McCracken decided once and for all to get out of doing a chore he hated: checking the fishing nets in Loch Ness every morning at 5:00 a.m. sharp. Sean made up a story about being attacked by a monster in the lake, hoping Uncle Patrick would see that he had been psychologically scarred and could no longer be expected to go out on the lake to check the nets. Sean told him the monster had grabbed his leg and nearly pulled him out of the boat as he was checking nets on the south side of the lake.

Sean knew his uncle well enough to know that he would want to see the monster for himself. Uncle Patrick, as Sean had expected, said, "I've been checking nets for over 50 years and I've never seen any monster."

Sean countered with, "If you don't believe me, I suggest you go see for yourself."

"Okay, I will," said Uncle Patrick. "I'll be there bright and early tomorrow morning checking the nets and waiting for your so-called 'monster.'"

The next morning, Sean woke up before Uncle Patrick and ran to the south side of the lake. He waded in until he was almost under the water, then cut a long reed to breathe through. He knew his uncle would have to dangle his legs over the boat in order to check the nets, and when he did, Sean planned to grab a leg and pull as hard as he could.

Sean waited under the water by the nets until he saw his uncle's legs dangling from the surface. Then he swam up and pulled on one of his legs as hard as he could. When he heard Uncle Patrick yelling "Help! Help!" he knew he had convinced him there was indeed a monster in the lake, so he let go and swam away, surfacing among the tall grasses where he could hide. He watched as his uncle quickly rowed the boat to shore, jumped out, and began running back to the house. Uncle Patrick told everyone his story, and soon the whole town was talking about "Nessie," the name Uncle Patrick had given the "monster."

From then on, Uncle Patrick never made Sean check the nets. Uncle Patrick didn't check them, either. Instead, Uncle Patrick assigned the chore to Sean's younger brother, Ian. After about a week of checking nets, Ian came back one day with a story about a monster, complaining that he was also afraid to check the nets.

Suddenly, without thinking, Sean burst out with, "He's lying!"

"And how would you know, laddie?" asked Uncle Patrick suspiciously.

Sean eventually had to admit what he had done. Uncle Patrick was furious, and demanded that Sean go to the village and tell every single person what he had done. Hence, the phrase, "You're pulling my leg," was born.

Incidentally, some of the villagers refused to believe the story, figuring Sean was making it up to put them at ease, and that's why the legend of Nessie lives on to this day.

95. The ringleader was arguing with the clowns again. Not one clown would agree to ride the lion "like a horsie," as the ringleader had suggested. Dabby the Clown explained to the ringleader that a lion was in no way like a "horsie" and that the trick was much too dangerous. Slappy the Clown also spoke up, saying the trick would not only be dangerous to the rider but might hurt the lion, too.

"Oh, nonsense," said the ringleader.

Rippy the Clown shot back with, "If you think it's so easy, maybe you should do it."

The ringleader replied, "I would, but it's not in my job description."

96. "Icky" is stepping barefoot on a freshly chewed wad of Bubblicious.

"Icky" is when the leftover meatloaf in the Tupperware at the back of the refrigerator is green and growing hair.

"Icky" is maggots hatching out of the fish guts in the bottom of the garbage can.

"Icky" is when your brother decides to wear the same Chicago Cubs sweatshirt every day for a month without using deodorant.

"Icky" is when your Big Guy Burger arrives with slimy, wilted lettuce and a hair hanging out of the bun.

97. Extensive research on a cure for hiccups has concluded that swallowing a half-cup of seawater followed by a cinnamon roll will instantaneously stop this annoying affliction. According to Dr. Philip C. Wrangler, the cure for hiccups may sound a bit unbelievable but it certainly works. He says he has begun advising his patients with chronic hiccups to follow the seawater and cinnamon roll cure and has had amazing results. "It really works," says Dr. Wrangler. "Apparently the seawater acts as a moistening agent for the diaphragm, relaxing the muscle. Then the cinnamon in the cinnamon roll stimulates the diaphragm one last time, essentially interrupting the hiccup cycle. Finally, the dough from the

cinnamon roll refocuses muscle activity in the stomach, diverting stimulus away from the diaphragm."

98. Bartholomew arrives home from his job as CEO of Yuppie Records, starts to brush off his camel hair coat, but then remembers he has a butler to do such things. He calls for Geoffrey and sits down as the butler brushes the coat and hangs it in the walk-in coat closet. Then he has Geoffrey slip off his Italian leather shoes and wipe them with a chamois cloth before putting them in his walk-in shoe closet.

    After changing into a cashmere work-out suit, Bartholomew goes to the kitchen to ask his personal chef to prepare dinner. He requests lobster thermidor with a salad of imported salad greens and French cheese. While waiting for dinner, he retires to his home movie theater with a glass of champagne.

99. The ocean would look red, since its color is a reflection of the sky. All maps would, therefore, have red oceans.

    The phrase, "blue skies" would never appear in the dozens of songs and poems it appears in today.

    Romantics would never utter: "Your eyes are as blue as the sky."

    No one would ooh and aah over red sunsets, since a red sky would be nothing special.

    Sailors wouldn't be able to distinguish between a red sky at night or a red sky at morning.

100. That low-slung little pooch of yours certainly has a unique and eye-catching haircut. And what a solid, sturdy little guy he is! His legs may not be overly long, but they certainly do get him around. And, my, what discriminating taste he has! He is *very* particular about what he eats. You'll never have to send him for training in assertiveness, either. The little guy isn't at all shy about letting you know what he needs or wants, or even when he is displeased about something. And he's smart. When he wants attention, he's bright enough to show you clearly what he wants! What a pooch!

101. The chicken crossed the road to feast on delicate strands of wheat.
    The chicken crossed the road to escape the farmer who was chasing it with an ax.
    The chicken crossed the road to elope with the rooster of her dreams.
    The chicken crossed the road to seek her fortune at the farm down the road.
    The chicken crossed the road to escape the representative from Chicken Nuggets R Us.

102. My new puppy is THE most adorable little thing. She has the cutest little paws, especially with the pink nail polish I use on her. She looks so precious in her little lace sweater and bow—they PERFECTLY match the pink nail polish. She is so cute I just want to squeeze her in a big hug CONSTANTLY!

    I got her a little china plate for her puppy chow. I take her for walks twice a day with her rhinestone leash that matches her rhinestone collar, and I'm just SO proud when people stop and admire her. I also got her a pink velvet puppy bed to sleep in when I'm gone. At night, she cuddles up on the pillow next to my head. It is SO sweet! I am the luckiest girl in the world to have found this little darling!

103. The orfinbellydorper is a highly sophisticated device used to attract salamanders. The orfinbellydorper impersonates a salamander sunning itself on rocks during the summer and sends out a slight vibration to signal to other salamanders that the area is safe. Switch the orfinbellydorper on and place the device on a rock in the sun. Soon you will enjoy seeing many salamanders sunning themselves next to the orfinbellydorper.

104. I have to walk past a creepy building on the way to school every day. The building is four stories tall with windows and doors that are boarded over. Most of the paint has worn off the building, and the porch has rotted boards and holes in it. Some people think the building is haunted. Strange lights appear inside at night, and strange sounds come from the building, too—moaning, screams, whistles. Once I even heard a yipping sound coming from inside. What kind of building yips? I get goose bumps whenever I am near it. I always cross the street to walk on the other side to avoid the creepy building.

105. What did the police officer say to the lady who was double parked while she ran into the bank for just a minute to get some cash before taking her granddaughter shopping at the new retail center?

Hit the road,
Or be towed.

106. What did the soccer mom say when giving her son James a ride to school and James turned the radio to his favorite station, which was playing a song with lyrics so offensive that she stopped the car in horror?

If that's a song,
That's WRONG!

107.   Never hug a porcupine.
     Never dye shorts in the turkey roasting pan.
     Never try for a close-up snapshot of a skunk.
     Never press "delete" when you're dealing with your hard drive.
     Never send eggs through the mail.
     Never eat the skin of a kiwi or a sweet potato.
     Never ride your bike in the dark wearing Goth clothing.
     Never buy a nosebleed seat at the baseball stadium, especially if you're prone to getting nosebleeds.
     Never drive at night without turning on your headlights.
     Never feed a crocodile cookies.

108. Jack and Jill were a brother-sister team of professional bobsledders who climbed up a hill near their mountain lodge to retrieve some water for their dog Skamp. Skamp was in desperate need of fresh mountain water—the water at the lodge just wasn't good enough for him.

     However, Jack tripped on his new boots and fell, rolling down the hill. Jill tried to grab him but tripped and came tumbling down after him. As Jack fell, his head slammed against a protruding tree branch, and he broke his crown. Though it looked serious, it wasn't that bad. A few stitches later, he was home. Jill, who had not been injured, welcomed him with hot tea and a disappointed Skamp, who still wanted some fresh mountain water.

109. I paid a visit recently to the local junkyard, searching for some spare parts for my wrecked car. Apparently a skunk had visited recently as well because the place stunk to high heaven. The proprietor, who appeared to be slightly drunk, managed to scrounge up a couple of spare parts covered in a thick layer of putrid smelling gunk. My stomach reeled and I promised myself that the next time I came searching for parts, I would not dunk day-old greasy donuts into my coffee on my way over.

110. Wow, I am furious! I cannot even believe that Blossom won't stop messaging me. Can't she take a hint? Does she really think that I am just going to forgive and act casual after she ate my piece of pizza, dropped AND broke my phone, got me in so much trouble that I had to stay for detention . . . which led me to also getting grounded! She is ridiculous. She is disrespectful. She just gets lonely and then tries to act nice after treating me like the gum on the bottom of her shoe. Also, if that isn't enough, Taco Bell raised the price on Mexican Pizza. Why can't there be anything that is just good and right in the world?!

111.   My, but isn't this festive looking—the colors of Christmas!
    This is certainly an interesting combination of ingredients.
    Why, I'll bet this is just loaded with antioxidants.

112. Brooke's front tooth is loose and she is anxious to lose it. She desperately wants the good tooth fairy to visit her room on the second floor. One evening, Brooke settles down with her favorite book, *Molly Moose and the Rusty Rooster Shoot Hoops,* and a big bowl of strawberry ice cream. Her dog sits at her feet and drools. As Brooke eats the cool treat, she hits her loose tooth with the spoon. "Oops," she thinks. She runs to the bathroom, kicks the door open, runs to the mirror, and tries to pry her tooth out. It still isn't loose enough. To boost her spirits, she goes to the front stoop to watch the neighborhood kids play in the street. She feels cooped up. She feels like pulling a hood over her head because the tooth fairy will pass over her house again.

113. I'm really sorry my mother planted pink geraniums in these pots on the porch. I really like red ones so much better, don't you? In fact, if it were me, I wouldn't plant geraniums at all. I'd choose some kind of wild flowers. I think wild flowers are so cool, especially when they're in the wild. But they would be cool in flower pots, too.
    I see you washed your car. It looks a lot better. My dad says you can tell a lot about a person by the state of his car. I guess "dirty" isn't a very good thing to say about a person, so I'm glad you washed it. Did you use that new car wash down on Seventh? I saw it was open, but I think it's fifty cents more than the one over on Ninth. Maybe it's better, though, or faster, or something. They must do something to justify fifty cents more.

At least you have a car. I sure wish I did. My dad says that having a car is a privilege, not a right, and as soon as I can pay for one myself, along with the insurance and gas, I can have one. Well, that's not going to be any time soon. I wish he was like Monica's folks. They bought her a car for her sixteenth birthday, and it wasn't even a clunker or anything like yours. I don't think she even knows how lucky she is.

Well, she's not lucky in all ways. She does have fat ankles. I mean, have you ever seen her in a skirt? Probably not, since she hardly ever wears one. That's because of her ankles. You can see them when she wears cropped pants or shorts in gym. They're bad, very bad. Very fat.

It's weird because the rest of her isn't fat. Maybe it's genetic or something…you know, like brown eyes or freckles. I'm sure glad I didn't inherit my dad's freckles. My sister did—but at least they aren't real dark like his. In fact, they're kind of cute.

Speaking of cute, I do think you're cute. Really cute. I guess that isn't the word guys like to hear. I suppose you'd rather hear something like "hot" or "handsome," but girls always say "cute," at least to each other. It's a good thing, you know.

Oh, you vacuumed the car, too. Cool! I like it a lot better. Last time there were all these little crumbs in the seat, like you had been eating potato chips or something. I guess they didn't leave little grease spots, though, so it must not have been potato chips. Maybe it was cookies…

114.   Hope will stay here.
         Send your blue book.
         Will your rose grow?
         Gwen came back home.

115. "Oh, man! That concert last night was righteous. My bro and I kicked it and didn't jam out of there until after midnight. It cost me plenty of dough to buy a hip t-shirt, and that bummed me out big time. Dude, I about wigged out when I saw the price, but it was so cool I had to have it. The next concert we go to, we gotta roll up in a tight car and hook up with our bros."

116. "How am I, you ask? Well, I could be a lot better. For one, my car has been in the shop for weeks. I've had to ride the bus to work every day. I hate riding the bus because it's so crowded. Also, I have to leave home two hours earlier than usual just to make it on time to work because the bus takes forever. So, I have to get up at 5:00 a.m. to make it to work by 8:00 a.m. That's not easy to do, especially considering that my new neighbors have been keeping me up late at night with their loud parties. And even if I could sleep through it, I can't because I have a pain in my big toe that has been keeping me up at night. The pain just keeps getting worse and worse. My doctor says it's the shoes I'm wearing, but I've been wearing the same style of shoes for years. I'm thinking of getting a new doctor. Good doctors are so hard to find, you know. I got rid of my last one when he started going on and on about hypochondria, and I knew the guy just didn't know what he was talking about."

Unjournaling © Taylor & Franci

117. I'm moving to New York City as soon as I can save up some money. I know I need to get a job to earn money, but the jobs in this town are so boring. Instead of getting one, I plan to hang out at the mall and play my guitar and pretend to be blind so people will throw money in my guitar case. It doesn't matter that I only know two chords and can't sing. People will still give me money because I'll try to look real pathetic. Then, as soon as I get enough money, my boyfriend, the Cruncher, and I are going to get going. He's pretty sure he can get a job on Wall Street if he doesn't wear the shirt with the skull on it. We hear that stock breaking pays real good. He thinks I'll get a job, easy, as a concierge at a fancy hotel, especially if I don't do the blind routine at the interview.

118.   Free verse:
         Wondering what makes the cake so moist?
         Wondering why the chicken salad is so yummy?
         Wondering why the potato salad is so scrumptious?
         Mayonnaise, the special sauce.

         Rhymed:
         Mayonnaise, mayonnaise—creamy stuff.
         Can't seem to ever get nearly enough.
         Hamburgers, hot dogs and grilled cheese too,
         Who cares if mayo's not good for you?

119. When Carter drove his beloved truck down the road, all people could see were the wheel hubs as he sped by. If they pulled up in a parking lot beside his truck, they were sometimes tempted to park right under it, for protection, if it was raining.
         Carter loved the bright yellow color of his truck, and he loved its shiny chrome roll bar and the handpainted "Yellow Fever" along the door, shooting flames toward the tinted windows.
         What Carter liked best, though, was the hot tub in the back. It was nestled beneath the side boards, hidden from view. When he drove down the road, steam rose from the truck bed, making it look as if his truck was really smoking. If he had friends in the tub, he sometimes liked them to howl out in pain, as if the truck were devouring them.
         Carter got a kick out of that.

120. The fumes emanating from my brother's room were so strong that my mother finally snapped. In a failed effort to show that she didn't care, she had let my brother be as messy as he wanted in his room. My mom is known for her super-sensitive nose, and finally she just couldn't take it anymore. She marched down to his room with a snow shovel and a barrel-sized trash can. She flung the mattress off of the bed frame and gasped. To her horror, she discovered rotten rinds of watermelon and a hard piece of pepperoni pizza sandwiched in the middle of an overdue library book. She sniffed out an Easter basket full of seven-month-old hard boiled eggs. She also uncovered athletic socks stiff with dried sweat and my brother's swimming towel, crawling with mildew. Last, but certainly

not least, my mom found an orange, green with mold, stuck inside one of my brother's basketball shoes.

121. Come on over to surprise Roy Robertson! Roy turns 60 on the Fourth of June 2006. Follow the enclosed directions to 1610 Fellows Court. 6:30 p.m. on the dot. Be sure to bring your most cherished dessert, too! Hope to see you there.

122. At Diamond Dog Sitting, your canine gets gourmet meals, bottled water, a cashmere dog bed, massage, and tender loving care.

123. I'll never forget that night my sister, your Aunt Ida, decided to elope with your Uncle Herb—only he wasn't your uncle then. He was just Herb. Actually, he wasn't your anything yet because you weren't even born! But anyway, it was a dark and stormy night, which is kind of ironic since Ida used to be afraid of the dark when she was a little girl. She would always run to my room when she'd wake up in the middle of the night, and I'd have to carry her back to her room and put her back to bed. She slept in a big four poster bed—actually, the one that's now in her and Uncle Herb's bedroom. You should have seen us trying to get that bed up the stairs when she talked her mom and dad into giving it to her. It took five of us three hours to get it in there, and even then we put several dents in the wall and stripped off a lot of paint.

    But anyway, Aunt Ida and Uncle Herb ran off to get married that dark, stormy night after Herb got laid off from his job as a used car salesman. He had been working at Ford's A+ Used Cars. I always liked Fords, though our dad didn't think much of them. My favorite was a Ford Thunderbird. I used to drive a T-bird back when I was a senior at Smallville High School, though my dad never could understand why I bought it. It was used, of course. Real used.

    But anyway, your Aunt Ida and Uncle Herb both ran off, and as soon as Dad realized she was gone, he took off in his Chevy truck. He didn't take a gun, and it's a good thing because he looked madder than I've ever seen him. He didn't track Ida and Herb down until three days later, and by then they had been married for three days and there wasn't much he could do. He was ready to accept the marriage, until he found out Herb didn't even have a job. Then he…

    Well, actually, I think I don't need to be sharing the rest of the story with you, at least not until you are a whole lot older!

124. Little Kaitlyn brought her shoes to Mom as they were getting ready to go shopping. "Oh, you found your shoes! Awesome!" said Mom, slipping them on Kaitlyn's feet. As they headed for the door, Kaitlyn picked up a toy that had fallen on the floor. "Awesome!" said her mother. Kaitlyn hopped into her car seat, and her mother said, "Awesome!"

    While they went through the store, with Kaitlyn strapped properly in the basket, Kaitlyn sang the ABC song. "Awesome!" said Mom. When Kaitlyn read "Count Chocula" on the cereal box, her mother said, "Awesome!" When she pointed to a doll and read "Malibu Barbie" on the box, her mother said, "Awesome!" When they pulled up to the checkout counter, Kaitlyn said, "I want to pay," and her mother said, "Awesome," letting Kaitlyn hand the cashier the money.

When Mom and Kaitlyn finally took their items and left the store, the cashier breathed a sigh of relief. "They're gone," she said. "Awesome!"

125. The dog Spot sat on the mat and chewed on his milk bone snack, while Boots the cat slept on her back with her feet in the air. When Boots woke up, she crept up to Spot and pushed her nose in his fur while she purred. Spot gave her a lick and knocked her off her feet, so she went to her bed and fell back to sleep.

126. Quenton felt queasy after eating quince and quail. He knew he should have eaten a sandwich at his favorite deli, but he had let his friend talk him into eating at the new quintessential gourmet place for lunch. He should have questioned the quality of the restaurant, but he didn't want to start a quarrel. On top of feeling sick, Quenton was also late for his meeting with Queen Ludmilla. He cursed himself as he quickened his pace. As a reporter, he had an appointment to meet with the new queen and take down quotes from her about the birth of her quintuplets. He began to quiver. That's it—I'm quitting for the day, thought Quenton. I'm going home to crawl under my quilt.

127. Mac practiced his smile while gazing at himself in the mirror. He tried a slow smile, a leering smile, a friendly smile, a knowing smile. Then he tried some nods—a slow, thoughtful nod, a satisfied nod, a happy nod, a powerful nod. He turned to the left, and then to the right, checking out his profile and smoothing down a stray hair. He winked, then turned to the side, winking again, only a little slower this time. Nodding his head then—a satisfied kind of nod—he smiled and turned off the light.

128. Son, when your mom and I met, she was a klutz. I'm sorry to be so blunt, but *klutz* is the only word for it. When we would go out dancing, she'd have to sit at the side and watch while I danced with others. If she went out on the floor, ambulances always had to be called.

BUT…one night your mom decided there was one dance she was sure she could do—the hokey pokey. I sighed and joined her on the floor. Well, she put her left foot in okay, and she shook it all about okay. Same with her right foot and her left arm and her right arm. I started to relax. But then she put her whole body in and she shook it all about. People started flying every which way as she knocked into them. Finally, the floor was cleared, and there was no one there but your mother. That's when I looked at her and knew she was one of a kind. She looked so adorable sitting there surrounded by people crying and grabbing their elbows and knees, I just had to ask her to marry me.

When our first child came along, we knew we had to name you in honor of that special dance. That, Hokey Pokey, is your history, and I hope you can be proud of it.

129. Want to know what single personal care item will make it less likely that girls will grimace and leap back when you try to kiss them?

Want to know the secret to my long, long marriage?

What helps, though doesn't cure, the effects of Uncle Roberto's garlic and onion tomato sauce?

Sissy, since you dropped your toothbrush in the toilet, do you know what you can use instead to help your mouth feel fresh?

What did Emory accidentally pour on his cut knee, instead of peroxide?

130. Late yesterday, police were called to the scene of an altercation at the Palisades Bar and Grille. According to eyewitnesses, a fight broke out during the Battle of the Grunge marathon concert being held at the Palisades this weekend.

Witnesses described a short, stocky man about 50 being chased by an assailant covered in cake crumbs and frosting. The assailant was allegedly pummeling the victim with drumsticks. According to the owner of the Palisades, the victim had entered the bar carrying a cake and accusing the performers of interfering with his cake baking business next door. The loud noises, the baker said, were causing his cakes to fall.

Bystanders report that, following a verbal dispute with a drummer, the baker threw the cake at the musician, prompting the drummer to attack the baker and chase him out into the street.

Both men were arrested and charged with disorderly conduct. The baker was reportedly treated at a local emergency room for minor cuts and scrapes.

131. "Why can't we just get some tattoos or something?" asked Joe uneasily.

"I already told you why." Amber looked at her watch.

"Remind me." Joe was not fond of rings, and couldn't envision himself wearing one every day for the rest of his life. He didn't even want to *think* about the commitment involved.

Amber had stayed up the previous night making sketches of the ring she had always dreamed of wearing. She knew the artist would agree that her design was perfect. She also knew that the man she was about to marry could not possibly be serious when he said, "Remind me." She decided to ignore him.

She said, "The ring maker will be here in ten minutes."

132. Penelope's Prickly Eggplant: Not your ordinary eggplant! Eggplant that has been steamed over a slow fire for hours has been sprinkled with kiwi skins, to give your tongue a wonderful prickly sensation. Served with a chili garlic sauce and freshly braised blueberries, this eggplant is one dish that will stick with you all day long.

Pickled Beef and Catfish Pie: A yummy Penelope original! Beef is stewed in dill pickle juice for several days to infuse the beef with the taste of dill, and then it is combined with fried catfish in a delicate prune and cabbage sauce. A lovely cornmeal crust is baked over all and then topped with homemade goat cheese and maraschino cherries. Truly a dish you will long remember!

Desert Dessert: A dessert sure to delight the pickiest of dessert lovers. A mound of thickly sliced jalapenos is smothered with a creamy caramel and pecan sauce and accented with freshly harvested Arizona cacti needles, offering our guests a Penelope original to be talked about for years.

133. Sad, sorry Stan stole a shabby shawl for Sweet Sally Sample so she's sure not to shiver at her shellfish store.

134. After taking the two-ton treasure to the tournament, a troubled trooper threw twenty turnips, trying to topple the turquoise trophy.

135. The lamp his nephew had built out of an old banjo sported logos from all the top hockey teams, topped with a Kool-Aid stained shade with sequins around the edge.

136. My Dear Gracie,

   I have watched you grow into such a beautiful cat and admire your zest for life and running up and down the stairs. I am happy that you are enjoying your life even though you can't go outside. You have been an excellent role model for the new kitty and I really appreciate your willingness to show him the ropes.

   Recently, you have acquired a new habit, a destructive habit that I am concerned about. The new rug in the living room seems to have grabbed your attention and sparked your interest. I have noticed you pulling on the nice rug and rolling yourself into it. Also, I hear you clawing on the rug as if it were your scratching post.

   Gracie, this rug is a wonderful addition to the household and I'd like for you to stop destroying it. How can I help you stop scratching and pulling on the rug? I hope we can find a solution to this new destructive behavior.

   Please let me know when you are available to discuss the situation. I look forward to working with you on this matter.

   All the best,
   Jill Jelly

137. "Okay, I did it," said the prisoner, "but I'm not sorry. I'm only sorry I got caught. I really wanted that jewelry and that plasma TV. I can't afford one, and I was only trying to get what I would have if the world wasn't against me."

138. When the beautiful woman in the fancy dress walked in to the crowded party, everyone noticed. She had nice skin, long hair, and long legs. She looked sad, however. She sat in a quiet corner all by herself.

139. When the statuesque model in the tight, sequined dress walked into the animated bustle of the party, everyone stared. She had glowing, bronze skin, flowing black hair, and legs so long and shapely that every woman in the room suddenly felt frumpy. As she sat in a quiet corner all by herself, she looked sad, with downcast, tear-filled eyes.

140. A middle-aged former hippie, still sad about having to give up his Volkswagen bus, plowed his PT Cruiser into a semi truck. The impact ruined the PT Cruiser and sent the former hippie to the hospital. A show-off taking his first turn at driving an ambulance drove too fast and ignored a red light. At the same time, a five-foot tall grandmother of twelve, who

was racing to the dance at the Eagles Club, also ignored the red light and hit the ambulance. Luckily, she survived the wreck, and so did the ambulance driver and the former hippie.

141. The new teacher sitting at her desk slowly looked up at the class. She cleared her throat carefully several times and then, in a voice so soft the students could barely hear her, said, "Excuse me. Excuse me." Students giggled a bit and kept right on talking. The teacher suddenly raised her voice, jumping up to reveal her black belt. She leapt onto the desk, and yelled, "DID I STUTTER?!"

142. A video game is a form of entertainment; people play video games to have fun and relax. Remember when you used to play stick-ball in the street? It's the same concept. Fun! The video game can be played on your smart phone, which is different from the rotary phone hanging on your kitchen wall. If the video game you are playing is about people building houses and your character is the electrician, you walk your character through the house by moving your thumb across the screen of your phone. If your character needs to pick up wire, cut wire, or hang lights, then you need to move your character around like a real person to finish the task. The goal of the video game is different for each game and is dictated by the people who write it.

143.   If you ever have the notion
         To try a tasty potion,
         A fruity combination
         Brings instant gratification.

144.   "So, what did you find out?"
         "No kidding?! Orange or red?"
         "What? I prefer orange."
         "Do you think there'll be any problems?"
         "Me, too. I think there might be limited access."
         "Canada? That might not be a bad idea."
         "Okay, I'll do it."
         "Not too long."
         "That depends on the rate."
         "Enough for three months."
         "I'll get right on it. Ciao."

145. If you could chew blue, it would taste refreshing and cool, like a gust of clean ocean air.

146.   One year and six months ago our basketball team managed to win, in Denver, the state championship tournament, a contest created by the previous coaches and dedicated to the idea that teamwork is the secret to success.

         One week and two days ago, the justice of the peace officiated at the marriage of my sister to a trapeze artist, changing the meaning of the phrase "love at first sight" to "love at first flight."

Eight years and many tears ago, my pet salamander passed into the great beyond and left me a broken mess, blubbering about my loss and vowing never again to take on the responsibility of a pet.

147. Our car would not have a very smooth ride, as it would clunk along the road with its square tires. Our CD player would have to be redesigned for rectangular CDs. Basketball, golf, volleyball, and softball would probably not be popular sports. Bagels and biscuits would be square. Hamburgers would be square everywhere, not just at Wendy's. Songs like "Rock Around the Clock" would make no sense.

148. On Thanksgiving day, we love to stuff ourselves with turkey, dressing, mashed potatoes, gravy, cranberries, and pumpkin pie.

149. My super hero is Proper Paula. Proper Paula intervenes when someone displays bad manners. She has the ability to cast spells that make people behave. For example, when people rudely yell at store clerks for no reason, Proper Paula appears and puts a spell on them that makes them apologize. When people butt into lines, Proper Paula is there to send them to the back, where they belong. Drivers who tailgate or cut people off suddenly find themselves stranded in a sputtering car, thanks to Proper Paula. She also appears when people talk loudly on cell phones in restaurants. She turns their cell phones into bread rolls, which they then must politely serve to others at their table. If they behave nicely for the rest of the meal, she will return the phones, but only if they apologize and promise to behave more considerately in the future.

And if someone should talk back to Proper Paula? She quite unceremoniously turns them into bed bugs.

150. The rich smooth gravy had a robust aroma and a creamy texture.

151. Madison skips into her classroom to share her good news. She beams at the kids—even those who always make fun of her—and laughs to herself. The other students can't help staring at her. What has happened to her normal scowl? Finally, one child asks, "What's with you, anyway? Have you won the lottery or something?"

Madison nearly sings her answer. "I'm going to Disney World! Next week! My dad has business there, and he's taking the whole family!" She twirls into her seat and glows. "I can't wait!"

152. Zeus can save worms.

153. The cat ate raw meat.
The cat's ears were wet.
The man heard the cat.
The cat ate cream.
The meat tastes raw.
The cat sat near the rat.
The cat ate treats.

The seats were red.

The seats were wet.

We heard the tram.

We saw the tram.

The rat went there.

The cat went where the rat went.

The man went west.

The Western man ate the meat.

The dream was sad.

The men traded the same dart.

The car started.

That car went west.

The man's tears were sad.

That man wears a tan hat.

The mat was wet.

The heated meat wasn't raw.

A rat darted near the ram.

A cat sat near the hat.

The theme was sad.

The men made darts.

The cat wasted the treats.

The men sent cards.

The ram ran near the stream.

Her heart was sad.

154. "It says here you wrote *Hamilton.* What's *Hamilton?*" asked King Tut.

"Oh, it's a musical I wrote," answered Lin-Manuel Miranda. "Many of the characters are portrayed as rappers."

"What's a musical? What's a rapper?"

"This might be kind of hard to explain," frowned Miranda. "Why don't we talk about *you?* Why did your people believe in mummification?"

"Oh, it's a long story," said King Tut. "I don't feel like answering. I'm a king, you know. I do what I want. So goodbye."

155. Hi! Yes, my boss is still as lame as ever. You won't believe the STUPID thing he did today! He can be so dumb sometimes. I mean, hello!! Earth to Mr. Byers! So, anyway, our receptionist was out sick today and I was busy taking orders over the phone, so Mr. Byers had to make his own copies. And guess what he did! He managed to run off 237 blank sheets of paper. What an idiot! I mean, it's like, how long has he been in business, and he still doesn't know how to make copies? Hello! I mean, a monkey could probably figure it out faster than my boss. But you gotta remember—this is the guy who tried to make

coffee without putting any water in the coffee maker. At least the firemen who came were cute—or should I say HOT!

156.   The storm flooded the highway.
        The deluge engulfed the town.
        Rain came in a torrential downpour.
        The snow accumulation was five inches today.
        As temperatures fell, rain turned to sleet.
        Hail stones fell from the sky, completely covering the ground, like snow.
        The rain didn't let up until the city was flooded.
        The sky sobbed rain, like Aunt Tilly when she discovered no one like her stuffed
            bell peppers.
        The clouds spit large, random raindrops.
        Like a magnet, the hot dirt seemed to pull the rain out of the clouds.
        The large, lacy snowflakes fluttered to the ground.
        The sky vomited rain in large, spontaneous explosions of water.

157. A white-faced mime robbed the Sunny Farms Assisted Living Center yesterday afternoon, without saying a single word. He got away with a large tray of tater tot casserole, Clarissa Finnegan's extra-large fuschia geraniums, and a supersized tin of Werther's candy.

    According to head nurse Emily Fenster, the mime was able to get past the front desk by winning the receptionist over with his especially good pantomime of climbing a rope. The receptionist thought he was part of that afternoon's entertainment. Since most of the residents were attending a Karate for Life class, the mime was able to slip in and out of rooms undetected after he left the receptionist's desk.

    Described as a male about five-and-a-half feet tall and 145 pounds, the mime was wearing a full-body black jumpsuit with a large white zipper and bow tie. His face was painted white with tiny black triangles under and over each eye. If you have any information on this or other local crimes, please call Crime Stoppers at 555-5555.

158. Mrs. Marvel never missed an opportunity. After a few minutes had passed and it was clear the the elevator wasn't going to be moving anytime soon, she decided to speak to the rather scary looking teenager and the older woman trapped with her.

    "So, how are both of you today?" she said brightly.

    "Duh!" said the teenager, showing a large stud in his tongue. Mrs. Marvel wondered if it matched the one in his eyebrow and the one in his nose. Did they come as a set, she wondered, like the pearl necklace and earrings Mr. Marvel had given her for their anniversary?

    "We're stuck in an elevator. How fine can we be?" continued the teenager.

    "I'm going to be late for choir practice, and I don't know how the choir is going to get along without my organ music," said the woman holding a hymnal. "But I suppose they are just going to have to make the best of the situation."

"Yes, that's the way the cookie crumbles," said Mrs. Marvel. "And speaking of cookies, are any of you familiar with Mrs. Marvel's cookies?"

The teenager rolled his eyes. "No."

"Yes," said the woman with the hymnal. "Someone brought them to our last church potluck. I didn't eat any, though. I heard they are *really* fattening."

"Well, you'd better avoid them then," mumbled the teenager, eyeing the woman's large hips.

"I wouldn't call them 'fattening,' per se," Mrs. Marvel hurried on. "Rather, they are a decadent treat to be enjoyed in moderation."

"Decadent treat?" sniffed the teenager.

This sales pitch wasn't going as well as Mrs. Marvel had hoped. "Yes, decadent treat. Sometimes we all need to spoil ourselves." She whipped open her bag. "My Oatmeal Chunkie Chews are a delicious treat for anyone, and they are only $15.00 a box!"

"Are you offering us some?" said the teenager. "I'll be happy to eat one and let you know how decadent a treat it is."

"Well, no, but I am offering to *sell* you a box."

The woman with the hymnal sighed and turned her eyes heavenward. "Some people would look at this as an opportunity for sharing," she said, "not for making money off of fellow sufferers."

"We're not suffering!" said Mrs. Marvel.

The teenager looked at her and scratched his tattooed earlobe. "Speak for yourself, lady."

159. Louise enjoys eating banana splits during movies. Others prefer peanut butter treats. Eating during movies causes really sticky mouths. Surely the viewer should expect drinks before cinema snacks. Coffee almost always brings relief.

160. Once upon a time, a mother was very tired one morning and just wanted to put on her comfy slippers and snuggle up with a book. Her three young children, however, had question, after question, after question that morning:

"Mommy, how come they don't put Elmo on the quarter?"
"Mommy, how does water get in the pipes?"
"Mommy, is Shaq a giant or are giants actually bigger than Shaq?"
"Mommy, why does the wind blow?"
"Mommy, how old do you have to be to be *old*?"

The mother's tongue soon felt numb from answering so many questions with her tired brain. Finally, when her son asked, "Mommy, how did you get so smart?" she decided *not* to tell him it was by doing well in school, always finishing homework, and going away to college. She looked outside, searching for an answer, and saw the mulberry bush in the backyard. "It came from running around a mulberry bush," she said. "Mulberry bushes are brilliant and wise... It can work for you, too, you know. If you go outside and run around the mulberry bush, singing, you will learn all of the answers to all of your questions."

The children decided to give it a try. Thankful, the mother poured a cup of coffee and curled up with her book, hoping for at least a few moments of peace and quiet.

161. A teenager to a parent: "Mom, I load the dishes in the dishwasher every night, make my bed every morning and take Buttercup for a walk every afternoon. I do all of this work around here, so the least you could do is pay for a new snowboard."

A bank robber to a teller: "Clear out your drawer and no one gets hurt. Believe me, this isn't just a finger I'm pointing under my jacket."

A woman to her ex-husband: "You are required—by law—to pay for our children's medical bills. Since Tory's nose job does qualify as a medical procedure, you *will* pay the bill!"

A couple to a loan officer at a bank: "Well, sir, we really need the money to finance a retreat for unwanted crocodiles. It's our dream."

A policeman to a driver: "Sir, pay the ticket now or go to court."

A dissatisfied customer to a store owner: "When I bought this turtle, you assured me that he would be a good companion. He's not. All he does is sit inside his shell all day, so I demand a full refund!"

A man who walked into a glass door to the concierge: "That's the second time this has happened. You need to put a sign on this door! And you are paying for my broken glasses!"

162. Andy drove all night to get home. By the time he reached the toll bridge, he needed to eat. Candy stashed in the glove box would not satisfy his hunger. Deciding to find a burger joint, Andy pulled off the freeway. Even though he loved tacos, he really craved a hamburger. Finally, a sign appeared for "The Best Burgers in the West." Growing hungrier just reading the sign, Andy pulled in to the parking lot. Happy and relieved at the same time, he grabbed his wallet and went inside.

"I'd like a burger, fries, and a vanilla shake, please."

"Just five minutes, sir." Kicking the counter with his foot, Andy wanted to cry because he was so hungry. Laughing and giggling on the cell phone, the woman ignored poor Andy.

"Ma'am, may I order?"

"Not right now, sir!"

"Okay, but I'm really hungry. Please may I order?"

"Quiet, sir!" Reeling from hunger and anger, Andy left the burger joint. Shame on her, Andy thought. That's the last time I go to the Wacky Wanna Burger! Until I eat dinner I can't drive another mile, he thought. Very grouchy and now starving, Andy couldn't think straight. When all hope seemed to be lost, a few bright neon signs flashed in the distance. "Xerox Copies" was a sign that glowed blue and made

Andy blue because he certainly couldn't eat paper, but then he noticed another sign, a sign that glowed red and read "Fast Food Fast." "Yes!" Andy yelled aloud. Zestfully, Andy skipped across the parking lot and to the counter to order some greasy fare that would keep him going for miles.

163.   I wouldn't marry you even if the entire future of civilization depended on us marrying and having children.

    I wouldn't marry you even if I had a choice between you and jumping into a vat of lemon juice with paper cuts all over my body.

    I wouldn't marry you even if you became the multi-millionaire owner of Ben & Jerry's ice cream and gave me a lifetime supply of Cherry Garcia.

    I wouldn't marry you even if you won the lottery and offered to buy me absolutely anything I wanted for the rest of my life.

    I wouldn't marry you even if I had no prospect of ever finding another man interested enough in me to propose and I knew I would have to spend the rest of my life alone and raising cats for company.

164. Susie sells seashells since summer's started, sometimes singing songs softly, sifting sand simultaneously. Seagulls swiftly sailing skyward swoop suddenly, so Susie startles. Since seagulls seldom scare Susie, she simply sighs, searching sandy spots, seeking several special shells, so she scarcely sees the seagulls.

165. Milford was happy to be warm and **dry** inside his car. As he put his seatbelt on, he looked out at the driving rain. The road was soaking **wet** just beyond his short driveway. "It's going to be a **slow** morning on the freeway," he said as he started his car and revved the engine. When the engine roared to life, it made a **loud** racket, but then it settled down to a **quiet** purr. He pulled out of the driveway and made his way to the freeway entrance as **fast** as he could. Once on the freeway, Milford found a safe and comfortable position behind a **large** semi truck. The truck was **high** enough to block the sheets of north-driving rain from hitting the windshield of his **small** car. When he reached the **low** valley of suburbs just before the city, he slowed down and began searching for his exit.

166.   I would choose a tiger for Dwayne Johnson because they are tough, and so his he.

    I would choose a poodle for Zendaya because poodles are beautiful and smart, and so is she.

    I would choose a cat for Simone Biles because she is graceful and always lands on her feet.

    I would choose a lion for Malala Yousafzai because she is brave.

    I would choose a mouse for Ariana Grande because she is tiny.

167. No. No, sir. I will not. I will not go. You can't make me go. Maybe you can go by yourself. Hank, please stop asking me to go. I have to work the day you go. It sounds like you will not go without me. If I go, how much would you pay me, Hank?

168. Dearest Mother, as you know these years tinged by pandemic have been long and lonely years—especially for someone my age. Online school and social distancing stunted my emotional development and empathetic growth. I have a solution: getting a pet cat. Caring for a little kitty will help to fast track my emotional skills that have languished in isolation. Not to mention, according to an online quiz, my love language is touch. A sweet kitty to cuddle and pet is exactly what is prescribed for a teenager like me. A cat is practically medicinal when you consider all that I have been through.

169. I love to eat at Avogadro's Number, a small quirky joint that features live music, including jazz, blues and bluegrass. Avo's has lots of wonderful food, including my favorite, hummus in pita pockets. It's a great place to get your food and music fix, all in one stop.

170. **OMG**

Oh Em Gee
How Ordinary,
Mundane,
and Generic
Or Maybe Go with
Optimally Magical Glamor
Like cosmic starlets waltzing with
Orion on the MilkWay across ten Galaxies
Or splashing with
Odysseus, Minotaurs and Gorgons
Or fighting dragons with
Ostentatious Mythological Gallantry
Oh My Goodness!
Is this Overabundance starting to be Obnoxious?
Do I sound Melodramatic and Maniacal?
Or Glowy like Gossamer?
Only My Guess
Or My Gracious
Oh My Gosh

171. Farley ogled Filmore's Taylor Swift cottage-core vibe complete with cardigan and snorted a snarl. Filmore threw her head back and cackled and then stared squarely into Farley's eyes and shook her head. Farley crossed her arms, raised her left eyebrow and defiantly smacked her lips as if to say "bring it on." Filmore closed her eyes in a "give me strength" prayer, then straightened her imaginary crown, and glided away like the queen that she is.

172. Computer geeks are a growing population of people that the world needs. Although we may call them "geeks," we probably should call them computer "experts" instead. They

would probably appreciate the change. After all, "geek" isn't exactly a title of respect, and we *do* respect them. Most of us would be lost without them. Think about that the next time you want a computer expert to fix *your* computer.

173. One cold, frosty morning in the middle of January, the coldest month of the year in the upper peninsula where natives wear triple thick long underwear and tourists wish they'd gone to Mexico instead, a century-old suspension bridge creaked and groaned in the gale force bitter north wind that howled across the frozen bay, before it twisted and broke away from its moorings, plunging with its lone, unknown pedestrian down into the icy, snowy darkness below, which leads us to the question with which we must now struggle, "Who was the lone pedestrian crossing the bridge that cold and frosty morning, and why wasn't he wearing any clothes?"

174. Olivia wants the world to know that she is an artist. She always wears a velvet, patchwork beret on top of her jet black hair. She wears emerald green eye shadow over just her left eye and violet over the right. She accentuates her cheekbones with glitter lotion and wears two large purple crystal earrings that look like they came straight out of my Aunt Millie's costume jewelry box. She always wears a long black turtleneck over a pair of ragged jeans that she has neatly doodled all over in blue ball point pen. She wears an old pearl necklace around her left ankle. Her fingernails are always painted an icy blue. And, on her feet, she loves to wear an old pair of loafers with buttons in the top slot, instead of pennies.

175. The yummy looking dessert tempted us when Mom took it out of the oven. The red fruit oozed out of the golden crust. It smelled so good we hoped she would let us try it. She did not. "No. It's for my book group meeting," she told us. We eyed it hungrily, but she didn't give in.

176. Advice to parents, from an experienced kid:
    1. Always allow your kids to pick out their own clothes because they are more up on the trends. You may cause your kid to look like a dork, without meaning to.
    2. Always allow your kids to talk on the phone. Sometimes phone calls can be about very urgent matters.
    3. Always give your kids an allowance, especially when they remember to unload the dishwasher after school without being reminded. Kids need to have money of their own.
    4. Always make sure to get your kids to basketball practice on time. If they're late, they may have to run laps, which isn't fair since it wasn't really their fault they were late in the first place.
    5. Always remember that your kids already feel bad when they mess up. You don't have to yell at them and make them feel worse.
    6. Always let your kid use you for an excuse. Sometimes it's easier for kids to say, "My mom won't let me," than, "I don't think I should."
    7. Always respect the different music choices your kids may make. Your kids may not like your music, just like your parents probably didn't like yours.

8. Always look for good things in your kids, even when they are really screwing up. Nobody is all bad.
9. Always remember that your kids could be a lot worse than they are.
10. Always be patient with your kids. If they already knew how to do everything right, they wouldn't need parents.

177. Woe is me. I got my wisdom teeth out last week and I've been eating mashed potatoes and applesauce for every meal ever since. My jaw hurts constantly; all I can do is sit around and watch television. When my friend came over to check up on me, I couldn't open my mouth wide enough to yell to her to make sure the cat didn't get out, and sure enough, it ran out. My poor, poor lost kitty was out in the cold all alone. I had to spend the afternoon walking around looking for her, and my jaw hurt something fierce! Finally, I found her, but I was so tired by then that I had to take a long nap when I got back home. When I woke up, there was dried drool down my chin. It was gross. I wonder if my jaw will ever be normal again.

178. Forget what you've learned in science class. The real reason that leaves turn brown in the fall has been kept well-hidden for hundreds of years, but now you can know the truth. A colony of beings called Metarbillatastiks, who live just on the outskirts of the center of the Earth, turn leaves brown in the fall by directing heat from the Earth's core up through tree roots. The heat reaches tree leaves and slowly bakes them until they wilt and fall off. The Metarbillatastiks use the dead leaves as fuel to stoke the heat in the Earth's core. They need to keep the core hot in the winter, or it might freeze. So, in the fall, Metarbillatastiks emerge on the Earth's surface to collect dead leaves in the wee hours of morning when no one else is around. They collect the leaves only in unpopulated areas, so no one will notice and thus start asking questions. The Metarbillatastiks take the dead leaves back to the outskirts of the center of the Earth, where they shovel them into a series of furnaces, leading to the Earth's core. The dead leaves feed the fire and keep the Earth running smoothly through the cold winter months. Fortunately, the fall season provides enough dead leaves to keep the Earth running until the next autumn, when the Metarbillatastiks make their dead-leaf-collection journey again.

179.   Version #1: Next time you go shopping at Food World, get in line #13 and notice the cashier as she checks your groceries. She stands in one spot, slides each item across the price scanner and drops it into a bag. This is her routine, and she repeats it a hundred times a day.

   Version #2: Next time you go shopping at Food World, get in line #13 and notice the cashier as she checks your groceries. *She's the woman with long pink braids who hums and dances in place as she slides the items across the price scanner, pops them up into the air (except for eggs), and catches them in her other hand before tossing them into the bags like Lebron James shooting hoops.* This is her routine, and she repeats it a hundred times a day.

180. Wearing flip-flops and torn jeans, Rusty Fotel approached his favorite heavy metal band, anxious to ask the members a few questions. The guitar player offered Rusty a slice of cantaloupe after autographing a poster. Rusty, their number one fan, asked the lead singer why the band didn't play more often in his hometown of Wichita, Kansas. The singer replied, "It's too late to worry about a tour schedule. All I'm thinking about is my toothbrush, toothpaste and a good night's sleep." The band left Rusty standing alone in the dark parking lot. He switched on his key ring flashlight and made the trek back to his car, questions unanswered.

181. slushy
slushy: unkempt in appearance; lacking neatness
slouphy: unable to make up one's mind; wishy-washy

The young boy stomped through slushy puddles on his way to school. When he arrived, his teacher stopped him in the hallway. "Your shoes are a mess, your coat is muddy, and your shirt isn't tucked in," she said. "Why are you so sloushy today?"
"What's it to you?" he asked rudely. He didn't care if he was sent to the principal, who was so slouphy that he could never make up his mind to punish anyone.

182. The last few seconds were suspenseful. The score was tied. Our star basketball player almost scored. Then the other team stole the ball. Luckily, they missed their shot. Then our team had another chance. We could win the game. Our star player had the ball. The last second was intense. He jumped high and slammed the ball, scored, and we won!

183. Bob Langowski is the king of kielbasa. He is known all over the Midwest for his speciality sausage making. As you can imagine, being around so much delicious sausage has made Bob a rather extra large man. The only thing larger than Bob is Bob's appetite. In fact, every Friday night Bob takes his wife Minnie to the Hungry Farmer restaurant out on Highway 50. And, every Friday night, Bob takes on the Enormous Ernie Challenge, which challenges any customer to eat a two-pound steak; three baked potatoes with sour cream, butter and bacon; a bowlful of creamy cole slaw and five pieces of Texas toast. If a customer eats all of this, by himself, he gets the whole thing for free. If he can't eat it all, he has to pay the $30 price. Just one look at Bob Langowski, and you know that he never has to pay for his meal at the Hungry Farmer restaurant.

184. Grandma Dorothy is a neat and orderly person. Her house is always impeccably clean. Every knick-knack in her house sits on a doily.
When she's out and about in town running errands or visiting friends, she always wears a hat and a shawl. "You can never be too dressed up!" she says. When she sees a man wearing a suit, she always comments, "He is quite a snappy dresser."
Grandma Dorothy doesn't like mess or chaos. When her grandchildren come to visit, they are not allowed to go anywhere in her house except for the kitchen. Grandma Dorothy insists that they sit quietly at her kitchen table and color in coloring books.

Grandma Dorothy does like to have fun. Every month she goes to the dance at the senior center. She always wants to dance with Mr. Birmingham, but she refuses to break her rule: "A woman should never ask a man to dance."

185. Sputter, Sputter, Little Car

Sputter, sputter, little car,
I know why you can't go far.
Your tires are bald, your engine's shot,
The miles you've gone add up to a lot.
Sputter, sputter, little car,
I know why you can't go far.

If someone drives you way too fast
They'll end up in a body cast.
Your rear axle's rusty and your brakes are bad,
Your overall condition is terribly sad.
Sputter, sputter, little car,
I know why you can't go far.

I wish you luck on future trips,
But sadly, I'm predicting drips.
Your radiator's leaking, after all.
You really need a mechanic's house call.
Sputter, sputter, little car,
I know why you can't go far.

186. dord: little figure that attaches to the dashboard of a car; the head usually bobbles.

I can't wait until I get my own car, even though it will most likely be my grandpa's old Fiat that only runs half the time. I wish I could be cool like my big cousin Frank. He bought this junky old car, and he has totally fixed it up. He painted it this iridescent color that looks green, but when you move, it looks blue. He hooked it up with these hydraulics that make the car hop. The dashboard is covered in a turquoise carpet with the name "Frank" embroidered in it. A little chihuahua dord sits on top of the dashboard, and its head bobbles like crazy when Frank uses the hydraulics.

187. objurate: to reproach or denounce vehemently
scrivener: a notary
predormition: period of semi-consciousness that precedes actual sleep
scrophularia: a family of plants comprising the snapdragon, foxglove, toadflax, etc.
voluminous: having or marked by great volume

My mom was super mad at me when I brought home my report card with a "D" in English. I could tell she was super mad because when she gets super mad, she uses really big words that no one understands. After she read my report card, she said,

"You're in voluminous trouble, young man. But before I objurate you, I have to go to the scrivener. While I'm gone, I want you to water the scrophularia and take out the trash. When I get back, I'm going to enjoy a nap, so be quiet and don't disturb my predormition. After my nap, you're going to get an earful about your performance in English class."

188. Eleven rides her bike so fast and hard that she loses track of where she is going. When she finally stops pedaling, she doesn't recognize where she is. Nothing looks familiar. Even the sky looks weird, kind of greenish with angry clouds. She is out of breath and wishes that her friend Mike was around. She has a sudden pang of hunger and remembers that she has a melted Three Musketeers candy bar in the pocket of this ridiculous pink dress.

    As she licks the melted chocolate off the wrapper, she looks around the road and into the horizon. She needs a plan where she can be safe, but that doesn't mean that she has to go back into the middle of town where she was being teased for her shaved head. She glimpses a gas station in the distance and decides to ride her bike there to look for a bathroom. She wants to wash the tears, grime, and chocolate from her face. She would like to find a phone booth but she doesn't have a dime. She wonders if she can call Mike's house with a collect call, which could be risky if his mom answered the phone.

    As she gets closer to the gas station, it looks empty but open. Just then an electric burst of thunder invites a heavy hard rain. The rain hits hard and cool, but it feels good. Her bike is harder to pedal in the puddles and the mud. The bathroom is locked and she would have to go ask for the key, but she worries that she looks even worse than before and decides to wait out the rain up against the side of the gas station.

189. ka-bluie, hah-tue, aw-tyu, eh-hoo, ka-chumpf

    Mayor Jones has the worst allergies you can imagine. In springtime, he *hah-tues* all day long from all the pollen in the air. The scent of flowering trees is the worst for him. One whiff brings on a big *ka-bluie*. It doesn't get better for him in summer. Anyone going into his office building hears repeated *aw-tyus* resounding down the corridors. Then in fall, he's bothered by all the dry weeds and mold flying in the air. He *eh-hoos* constantly. When winter finally comes, it's the cold dry air that gets to him. You can tell he's nearby with the sound of a little *ka-chumpf* as he goes about his business.

190. Cornflake lovers, beware! Some evil people are taking boxes of cornflakes, implanting tiny chips in them, and then putting them back on the shelves. Then they monitor the chips, which are able to take a photograph of the person eating the cornflakes. Then they use facial recognition technology to search the internet, find a name that goes with the face, and match that face to an image of the credit card. It's hard to explain how it works, but I just know you need to avoid cornflakes and buy Wheaties instead.

191. Willard the Wizard was an irrational environmentalist who thought he could solve all the world's environmental problems in the wackiest ways. First he waved his wand and turned every car on Earth into a flower. Then he became worried. Would there be enough bees on the planet to pollinate all of the new flowers he had created? In an instant, however,

he came up with a solution: He decided to turn people into bees so that they could pollinate the cars-turned-flowers.

As Willard mulled over his plan, a young girl named Bea was on her way to school. She was skipping along, excited to get to school so she could show her teacher the wonderful job she had done on her assignment. The other kids made fun of her for being a teacher's pet, but Bea didn't care. She was going to go to law school someday.

Suddenly, a wave of blue and orange light passed in front of Bea's eyes. Her backpack dropped to the ground, along with her shoes and clothes. Bea felt strange. She heard a buzzing noise she couldn't escape.

She realized that she had an overpowering urge to become something else—a bee. "What is happening to me?" she wondered. *Bea had never before wanted to be a bee.*

And then, after another wave of light passed in front of her, she realized the unthinkable. She *was* a bee! It took her a moment to adjust, but soon she was just fine with her new state of bee-ing. As she admired her giant stinger, she decided to go track down those kids in her class who always chided her for being a teacher's pet.

192. There it sits in the YMCA parking lot—an extra large van with navy blue stripes wrapping around it. One peek in the window reveals two car seats, snot-smeared windows, empty juice boxes and melted crayons in the cup holder. The passenger's seat is covered with a week's worth of school projects, including a collage made out of Fruit Loops. Some of the Fruit Loops have been nibbled off. A soccer ball, two tennis rackets and two pairs of arm floaties are on the floor.

The driver of this car is inside the YMCA teaching an aerobics class. The class is the only thing that keeps Tiffani from looking like the mother of five children, from a seven-year-old down to two-year-old twins. She is still in good shape, despite the thousands of fat-laden grilled cheese sandwiches she has had to scarf down with the children, along with the special grape Kool-Aid that she makes with only half of the sugar.

193. Emerson wears a ball gown made completely from recycled car tires and a feather-like boa woven from recycled bicycle tubes. Her hair is bleached platinum and looks greasy. It is topped with a crown made of recycled bicycle spokes. Her makeup is gray face powder but with gold lipstick and mascara. She has a black smudge under her right eye. Her shoes are shiny gold platform boots. She wears yellow diamond earrings on loan from Tiffany's.

194. Arnold's approach to landscape design is truly unique. He has a real passion for lawn ornaments and certainly uses them freely. He especially loves ceramic pigs, painted a very eye-catching shade of purple. Currently, he has 73 of them, in various sizes.

He also prefers to keep the holiday spirit alive all year round with his ambitious light displays that cover every inch of his house, as well as all the trees, shrubbery, and lawn ornaments—including the pigs.

Arnold believes in keeping his neighbors informed. He always tells them, via a bullhorn, when he is going to his mailbox to check his mail. He notifies them, with

• •

polite notes taped on their doors, whenever he believes they have done anything to annoy his ceramic pigs, which seem to take offense rather easily.

195. George Weasel approached the woman who was looking over the cars at his dealership.
"I'll bet you want something sporty," he winked, giving her an appreciative once-over.
"No," said Fiona Blunt. "I want something practical."
"Well, practical is okay, but you really look like someone who needs something a little more upscale. Maybe something blue to match those gorgeous eyes of yours."
"I was thinking of a mini-van."
"You don't belong in a mini-van! You're much too sophisticated for that. How about this hot little convertible?"
"How about you telling me where you expect my four kids to ride in something like that? And how you expect me to buy *anything* from someone with your lame lines?" She turned and walked out of the dealership.

196. "Why don't you learn how to talk to a rooster?" Cindy yelled. Her brother was clearly no help in coaxing the rooster into the cage. How were they ever going to get her precious Doodle-Doo to the vet? His comb was looking pale, and he had stopped crowing every morning at 4:30. Sometimes he was as late as 8:00 a.m., and even then the crowing was pretty feeble. He was a sensitive rooster, and one that needed to be handled gently. As she held the cage door open again, her brother bellowed, "Come here, you stupid rooster." That was it. Cindy had had enough of her brother's rough ways. She slugged him.

197. Pat is a 14-year-old boy who lives with his mom and dad. Pat likes videogames, so he was recently disappointed that he didn't receive the game Killer Commandos for his birthday. His parents told him it was too violent, and that they were worried it might adversely affect him. He was pretty darned sure they were wrong. He was also pretty darned unhappy.
Pat tends to sulk when he's unhappy. He mumbles and mopes and slams doors. He's rude to his sister. (Actually, he's rude to his sister even when he isn't unhappy.) His parents roll their eyes and try to ignore him, unless he becomes too obnoxious. Then they send him to his room, just so they don't have to deal with him.
Last Sunday afternoon, Pat visited his grandmother, as usual, and she made him very, very happy. She gave him a special birthday present—$50.00. With what he had already saved, he knew he had enough to buy Killer Commandos. When he got home, he told his parents he was going to ride his bike to the mall.
Unfortunately for Pat, his sister spoke up. "I see you have an envelope from Grandma. How much money did you get?"
"None of your business," said Pat.
"I'll bet it's enough to get you interested in riding your bike to the mall. What are you going to buy?"
"None of your business," said Pat.
"It isn't Killer Commandos, is it?" said his sister.
"None of your business," said Pat.

His parents finally tuned in to the conversation. "Pat, if buying Killer Commandos is your intention, you'd better get that out of your head. You're not allowed to have Killer Commandos, and that's final."

"I can't believe this!" yelled Pat. "This is so lame! What right do you have to tell me what to do?"

His parents looked at him and sighed. "We're your parents," his father said. "Live with it."

Pat stomped upstairs.

"Does this mean you're not going to the mall now?" his sister called, ever so sweetly.

198.   I'll bet he could lift a truck if he wanted to!
Look at that six-pack!
I'll bet he runs marathons.
He should be a professional bodyguard.
All he needs is a handle-bar mustache and he could join the circus as a strong man.
You wouldn't want him as an opponent in an arm wrestling competition.

199.   Rock-a-Bye-Baby.
Safe in my arms.
I will protect you,
keep you from harm.
I hold you tightly,
next to my heart.
Nothing will ever
tear us apart.

200.   The Applewood Estates Homeowners' Association has the personality of a fussbudgety old maid in a movie from the 1950s. The group has its nose in everything. Want to paint your fence white? It has to decide if you have chosen the right white for the neighborhood. In its opinion (and it is never wrong!), all homeowners should choose White Effervescence, never Eggshell or Snow Symphony. If you should forget to get the Association's approval, well, you will have to pay the consequences. Rules are rules. You will have to repaint, unless, by chance, you have chosen White Effervescence.

201.   *Hat Head Helper* is a better name than *Unsquish* for Kai's company because squishing happens to a lot of things, not just the hair on your head. Hat Head Helper is more specific.

Hat Head Helper is the latest product developed to fix that squashed look when you take your hat off. It is especially useful in cold winters when a stocking cap is often necessary. Take the hat off and Hat Head Helper will instantly take away that smashed look and return your hair to normal. How? Just keep the handy, Chapstick-sized Hat Head Helper in your pocket. When needed, whip it out, turn it on, and quickly hold it over your head. The waves coming from Hat Head Helper will activate instant memory in your hair strands and cause them to revert to however they looked before the hat bent them out of shape. Unbelievable? Try it. You'll be glad you did.

202.   Jamal ate some cookie *dough*.
    Delaney saw and cried, "No, *no*!
    I heard you blow your nose and *cough*,
    and that is just a real turn *off*.
    My advice to you is *tough*,
    But no one wants to eat your *stuff*."

203. Making your bed can cause you to lose a toe. Here's what happened to someone my friend knows. She was innocently making her bed when she saw an Amazon truck pull up. She didn't want porch pirates to take the box, so she hurried to the front door. Unfortunately, she was still wearing the giant shark animal slippers she got for Christmas. When she opened the door, her dog got out, and she had to run after him. The Amazon delivery person saw her giant shark slippers and started laughing. She turned to give him a dirty look and tripped over her dog. One animal slipper flew off as she fell. She got up, holding on to the dog, and limped over to the first step, where the slipper had landed. As she reached it, the dog tried to twist out of her grasp, and she wasn't paying attention. She managed to bump into the step with her bare toe, breaking it. The toe got infected, and eventually it had to be amputated. It just goes to show you, making your bed in the morning could mean losing a toe! Be careful!

204. Mr. and Mrs. Mancini's multilevel mansion has magnolia siding and maroon shutters. It sits on Mockingbird Lane in the middle of Millford Mill, Maryland. It is surrounded by magnolia and maple trees with marigolds lining the walkway to the midnight blue door. Their view of the misty mountains is magical.

205. People roll their eyes when I talk about my new podcast, "Things I Do That You Should Copy." They think my ideas belong in the last century, but they are wrong. Here are the topics I cover in my first episode:

- How to fold a towel the *right* way. I learned this from my mother who learned it from *her* mother, who learned it at least 100 years ago, and it's still true!
- How to unwrinkle clothes without using an iron. I learned about this one from a traveling business woman at the airport, after I had already wasted ten years not wearing clothes that were wrinkly and lived in the back of the closet.
- How to get at least three good blows out of a Kleenex using all four corners.

206. As Ursula ate her Froot Loops, she began to feel queasy. She set her spoon down on the table and got up to take some ibuprofen. Suddenly, she fainted. When she woke up, she was in an unfamiliar room. Her breakfast was with her, and her shoes were off and under a table. She had fallen onto the floor. She got up, drank the milk, and put a spoon in

her back pocket. She fainted again when she saw two shadows that looked like aliens approach her. While she was out cold, they returned her to her apartment.

207. Nothing soothes the cruel world quite like gravy. At Good Gravy, you can enjoy a ladle-full of comfort on your favorite foods from fries to apple pies. Come on in and try gravy on pancakes, hamburgers, and even ice cream! I am Garvey, owner of Good Gravy. I am so confident in our adventurous use of gravy that I guarantee you will love it or I will give you your money back. The only question left is: Brown gravy or white gravy?

    Good Gravy, where *everything* is gravy!

208. From Stella, about Cosmo's musical taste:

> If sadness had its own music fan club, Cosmo would be the president. While he loves to joke and appears to be a very jolly person, he has no limit to the depths of despair on his Spotify. If there were a theme song for his life, I would say it is "The Worst" by Jhené Aiko. He plays "Brutal" by Olivia Rodrigo on repeat every morning while he gets ready for school. I have even seen him (it's puzzling for sure!) actually dance to "Everybody Hurts" by REM. His music is gross, sad, and dramatic all wrapped in a ball.

From Cosmo, about Stella's musical taste:

> Sticky sweet, painfully perky, agonizingly amiable. This is how I would describe the ridiculous music taste of my sister Stella. Have you ever had a piece of candy that is so sweet that it kind of makes you gag? This is exactly what happens when I listen to any of her Spotify play lists. "Don't Worry Be Happy" by Bobby McFerrin, and Pharrell Williams' "Happy"? Yes, she is this obvious. She binge listens to ABBA. She blisses out to "Everybody Loves the Sunshine" by Roy Ayers Ubiquity. It is just cringy levels of embarrassing to listen to this kind of music when we are practically living in a dystopian science fiction novel.

209.
1. Separate the forks, knives, and spoons.
2. Put the silverware handles down.
3. Line up the coffee cups.
4. Line up the glasses.
5. Put all the plates vertically and facing west.
6. Popcorn popper lid should only go on the bottom rack.
7. Don't mix the chopsticks with the silverware.
8. Don't let the dog lick the clean dishes while you are unloading.
9. Rinse the cheese grater really, really well before putting it in the dishwasher.
10. Listen to music while loading and unloading the dishwasher. It makes the job easier.

210. Lola wakes up promptly every morning at 4:00 a.m. to the cheerful sounds of Barry Manilow's *Copacabana*. She spends her first 15 minutes unraveling herself from the gauzy

material that is wound dozens of times around her. She only gets a good night's sleep when she is wrapped up like a mummy. At 4:15, she does an invigorating 234 (her lucky number) push-ups while watching the weather channel. Lola then takes an ice cold shower, which she swears is enjoyable after the first icy shock wears off. At 4:50, she braids her long wet hair and coils the braids around her head like a crown. This means that she is ready for her 5:00 a.m. horse ride, and her team has already prepped and saddled her beloved horse Legend for her.

She briskly rides Legend across her vast property whatever the season. When she returns from the hour-long ride, Lola is ready for her hearty protein breakfast: two turkey sausage patties and two hard-boiled eggs. At 6:30, she pours herself a large cup of coffee topped off with oat milk and sits on her favorite velvet chair to check her Twitter and Instagram feeds. She only gives herself a strict 15 minutes to indulge in social media. Then she reads poetry by Rumi to cleanse her mind.

At 7:00 a.m., she meditates for 15 minutes in an unusually hot room. At 7:15, she unbraids her hair and takes a brief, scalding-hot shower. By 7:30, she is ready to get dressed for the day in the clothes her stylist has selected and laid out for her. At 8:00 a.m., her team quickly does her hair and makeup consistent with the carefree style that has made her famous.

211. Being bent over a cell phone: *mobilehunching*. Those people at the next table were *mobilehunching* through their entire meal at the restaurant.

Texting rapidly with the thumbs: *ambidextexting*. The speed of his *ambidextexting* was astonishing to watch.

Running into things because you are looking at your cell phone while walking: *textbumping*.

Jamal ran into a lamp post and two people as he *textbumped* down the street.

212. Because she had to bend down and pick up her phone, Hoshi realized she wasn't going to make it across the street in time before the light turned red, so she went back to the side of the street she started crossing from originally and had to wait for the next walk signal. Because she had to wait for another walk signal cycle, she was late to work. Her boss fired her because that was the last straw, as she had been late to work many other times before. She went home and was mad, so she threw a chair out of anger. The chair hit her fish tank, the contents spilled everywhere, and the fish ended up dying on the carpet.

213. A cat is like a heating pad. It can rest on your lap and keep you warm.
A dog is like a vacuum cleaner. It will suck up any food you drop on the floor.
A woodpecker is like a jackhammer because it puts holes in structures.

214. Calling all lovers of ooey, gooey oven-created treats!

Stop at our area at this weekend's street festival for a free sample of our three newest recipes. We will give out samples of our delicious toasted sandwich slices, our chocolaty dessert squares, and our chunky round sandwich wheels that are perfect for a schmear of cream cheese. You will find yourself astonished at how scrumptious all these new items are. Thank you for all of your support. Our little shop keeps expanding, thanks to your trust in our culinary talents!

215. Henry stared blankly at the huge television hung on the wall, never taking his eyes off the screen even when the station aired a commercial during a break in the football game. He clenched his teeth and his fists and banged his beer can on the coffee table. Whenever he banged the table, his wife would wince and cast sidelong glances at the neighbors watching the game with them. She kept jumping up and rushing to the kitchen to refill bowls of popcorn and chips. While the television blared, her son Dennis checked messages and emails on his phone, tapping replies. Finally, yawning, he put his phone down, closed his eyes and rested his head on the back of the couch.

216. An alien got out of the spaceship. He was green, pumpkin shaped, and had one eye. He was the size of a normal pumpkin. He made funny noises that made people laugh. He got out of the spaceship and crossed the street and got run over by a motorcycle. When he got up he was completely flat like a pancake. Everyone was laughing at him. In fact, the whole world was laughing at him. The alien saw his reflection in a store window and saw how funny he looked so he started laughing, too. And then he had to go to the bathroom so he ran to try to find one so he wouldn't pee on the street.

217. Drew Drake generally ran a road race every Thursday at a local race track, but in March he ran a race every Friday. He surprised everyone by coming in first in one of the races and setting a record. His running mates congratulated him warmly, and his girlfriend Ariana hugged him. His prize was a trophy, which he proudly carried to the restaurant where they celebrated his win. He loved the praise. He also loved the bacon cheeseburger and fries he ordered as a treat. He ate his burger and finished Ariana's. Then he got sick and threw up. (He earned $4800 for 48 *R*'s.)

218. • A cell phone and cereal both start your day. The cell phone alarm wakes you up. The cereal is your breakfast.
   • The cell phone and the cereal box both give you something to read while you eat.
   • Both can fill you up. The bowl of cereal fills your stomach, and the cell phone can fill up your brain with all kinds of images.
   • Both are things you don't want to drop.
   • Both can be customized to your own taste. For a bowl of cereal, you can use milk or cream, sugar or fruit, healthy brands, or ones that just taste good. Cell phones let you customize your ring tone, home page, and so much more.

219. • Disappointment is no dessert served with dinner.
   • Disappointment is having your favorite football team lose.
   • Disappointment is having a bad hair day.
   • Disappointment is when a friend cancels plans with you.

- Disappointment is being chosen last for a team.
- Disappointment is doing poorly on a test.
- Disappointment is when you break your favorite coffee cup.
- Disappointment is a rainy day when you planned an outdoor party.
- Disappointment is waiting for a train or plane that is delayed again.
- Disappointment is gaining weight when you don't want to.

220. After mowing the lawn I rested on the deck. There was a cool breeze blowing as I sat in the shade of the umbrella. My tall glass of lemonade was cold and refreshing. I kicked the recliner back and close my eyes, feeling a sense of accomplishment.

221. Penelope tweeted her break up letter, which was pretty rude. She loves to create unnecessary drama. This, of course, all happened just before her basketball game against the school from across town. The six foot center on the opposing team was her ex's sister. Needless to say, it was not surprising that the basketball game ended in a brawl.

222.
- Isn't it a great day? I rode my Harley to the office and enjoyed the fast wind in my hair.
- Good morning! Have you ever eaten bugs? I had a bug appetizer last night. Not necessarily yummy but super thrilling to try.
- Plans this evening? Me, too, but I am not at liberty to tell you about them—yet!

223. I have gathered you this evening to discuss the noble idea of chore rotation. I fear that my continual task of vacuuming is depriving you both of the opportunity to enjoy the distinct pleasure of pushing a Hoover over our plush carpet. I fear too that I am depriving you both of my other masterful skills in laundry, bathroom cleaning, and kitchen care. With this in mind, I humbly suggest that I have fulfilled my lifetime obligation to vacuuming and could be entrusted with a new chore of service to my family—not in addition to but *instead* of vacuuming.

224. Dear Million Dollar Investors:

Imagine a hot buttermilk biscuit slathered in fresh strawberry jam—not the usual kind filled with fake sugar and food coloring. Instead, imagine you could go to any store in America and buy a jar of strawberry jam just like my Grammy Gloria used to make in her old country kitchen using fresh farm strawberries. Yum! Jovon's Jelly Jam will let you do exactly that! It will deliver the kind of jam that hard working Americans deserve.

I have all of my Grammy's recipes and a line-up of amazing farm fruit suppliers. Just imagine all of the happy people at breakfast tables all over America if you invest in Jovon's Jelly Jam.

Sincerely,
Jovan

225.   Awake World
       Rocks Music

Makes Magic
Tells Story
Earth Spins
Trees Birth Roots
Moon's Orbit
Glows Light
Among Black Night
Space Dream Grows
Stars Spill Truth
Solar Rises
Takes Pulse
Heart Beats
Fresh Today
Alive

226. Chewy chewed the Chipotle chicken burrito with delight. His best childhood friend Chelsea preferred her Mama's chalupas with melty cheese to some cheap chain restaurant food, but she choked down a chunk of the burrito he'd ordered for her. Chewy rolled his eyes at Chelsea. He found her choosiness to be a bit challenging, but he just softly chuckled at his chubby childhood friend. When she started to chuck half a burrito into the trash, he grabbed it and ate it himself.

227. "Oh no! My aunt is in the hospital! I should probably go to the hospital to see her. Sorry, you will have to leave."
"I'm happy to wait here and keep an eye on the place until you get back."
"I don't need anyone to keep an eye on the place."
"Well, I could come with you to comfort you. This must be hard on you."
"No, thank you. Really. I'm going now. By myself. And you need to leave, too."

228. Becca's *vicious* dog, Pumpkin, *pulverized* the confetti birthday cake with fluffy pink frosting, and it made the whole party a *disaster*. While Pumpkin *obliterated* the cake, Becca shrieked, "Stop! Stop!" at the top of her toddler lungs.

229. • Pluto will forever be a planet and deserves to be a planet. You cannot un-planet a place.
    • We should have milkshakes for dinner every night because they are rich in calcium, and my bones feel brittle.
    • Hermione is the absolute best character in Harry Potter because she is magical and brilliant. Her knowledge of everything saves their lives more times than anything else.

230. Igor spends a lot of time looking into reports of UFOs. He is convinced that BIM-BB1 are coordinates to a residence on the planet Blimphon in another universe. He is signaling to the people—or whatever—there that he is friendly.

231. "Ugly haircut," Daiyu told her best friend. "You should have left it long."
    Cecily burst into tears. "Are you serious? You hate it?"
    "Absolutely," said Daiyu. "The shape makes your face look fat."
    Cecily ran off.
    "Hi," said her friend Desmond. "Watch this. It's so funny." He held up his phone.
    Daiyu looked at the video. "It's not funny at all—unless you are, like, five years old."
    "What's your problem?" Desmond said and walked away.
    "That was mean," said Lydia.
    "It was just the truth," said Daiyu, shrugging and walking into her algebra class. When class started, Mrs. Humphries caught Vanessa and Dakota whispering.
    "If you have something so important to talk about, would you like to share it with everyone?"
    "No," muttered Vanessa.
    "They were making fun of your high screechy voice," said Daiyu.
    "She's lying," said Dakota.
    "No, I'm not," said Daiyu. "And they were right. You have a very annoying voice."
    "And you are a very annoying person!" said Vanessa.

232. • School destroys creativity. Kids have to learn to look for the right response instead of thinking out of the box.
    • By eight, kids can read and write. They can use that skill to figure out what else they need to know.
    • Families would grow closer and be happier if parents didn't have to sit with kids and make them do homework every night.
    • Kids would be free to learn about what interests them, instead of what schools say they should learn about.
    • If they didn't have to go to school, kids could get jobs and help support their families.

233. • Touch: scratchy
    • Smell: pungent
    • Sight: sparkling
    • Hearing: whispered
    • Taste: bitter

Letitia saw the sequined dress *sparkling* in the window and *whispered*, "Yes!! I want that!"
    She hurried inside and asked to try it on.
    Standing in front of the mirror, tears came to her eyes. There was a *bitter* taste in her mouth because she realized she couldn't buy the dress. The price was right, but the sequins made it *scratchy*, and, even worse, the dress had a *pungent* odor she couldn't identify. It smelled so bad that she almost ripped the dress off.

234. At the Zenith Exposition that I experienced with my quirky quintuplet acquaintances in Quebec, we were told to expect an extremely exhaustive exam before we could exit the

Zoom session on "Blazing the Horizon with Acquired Quintessential Quotations." After a quick text query on where we might acquire a quality meal to quench our thirst and nourish our brain cells, we zipped over to Quinoa Express, a quiet brazier with a bizarre list of zesty, expensive meals. With our hunger quashed, the six of us left the quaint establishment and whizzed back to the Expo.

235. Five reasons for changing the title:

- The title is confusing. "Fluffy-Muffy" sounds like a name for a sweet little kitten or something. It's not a movie about a sweet little kitten.
- Most people have never heard of a menacing Madagascar hissing cockroach.
- No one knows where Madagascar is.
- The title is too long. Most successful movies have short titles.
- Cockroaches are just not appealing to anyone.

236. Five reasons Nakai gave for keeping the title:

- The title fits what the movie is about.
- Unusual titles attract people's attention.
- If people don't know what a menacing Madagascar hissing cockroach is, watching the movie will give them an opportunity to learn.
- Horror films are always popular, but none have been made yet about a Madagascar hissing cockroach. That will attract interest.
- My friends are all teenagers, and they like the title. It's good to appeal to teenagers because they spend money at movies.

237. Fabiana Brizzi, nicknamed "Fluffy-Muffy" by her parents, is an adorable, curly-haired toddler until she turns five. After being stung by a strange-looking bee at the zoo, Fluffy-Muffy turns into a Madagascar hissing cockroach whenever she doesn't get her way. At first her terrified parents keep this trait a secret and try not to say "no" to Fluffy. But when Fluffy starts asking for things like a new Porsche or 16 little sisters, they are unable to fulfill her demands. She turns into a cockroach that grows and grows with each "no," and soon she is roaming the town, creating fear and destruction everywhere she goes. Mr. and Mrs. Brizzi must go on a quest to figure out how to save their daughter and at the same time save the whole town.

238. From Mickey:

Amazing game! Hands down one of the best games I've played all year. It gives you the specs on your speed, stability, and at the end of each race, it gives you the specific information of that race (i.e., your tilt, the number of your stunt attempts, etc). The music is really cool. It also has good avatar choices—many more options than just the basic ones that most games offer. And the biggest reason I recommend this game is because it is available on all platforms!! This is huge! Being able to play on a digital device, Xbox, PlayStation, phone, and computer, is awesome! I can easily play with my friends now because of this.

From Morgan:

> This game is frustrating and a bit overrated if you ask me. You can only earn coins after you've completed five levels, so where's the incentive there? If you've never played the game, then it will take you a while until you're good enough to beat the first five levels. People won't stick with this game long enough to achieve the goal of defeating five levels before progressing to superior status. I say this game will be forgotten by next year. There is no incentive early on in the game and people will get annoyed. Also, there's no option for multi-player mode. Big mistake. People love to play *with* other people, so if that's not an option, then your game will not survive.

239.   "Oh, my," said Professor Percival. "This delectable creation is a titillating treat. It's akin to ambrosia, nectar of the gods!"

"Yeah, well, I like fruit salad better."

"Maybe this will help. Would you like to partake of a chalice of the fruit of the vine?"

"Sure," said Professor Penelope. "Merlot?"

"And be sure to save room for some gastronomical decadence at the end of the meal," Professor Percival advised.

"No, thanks. I hate sweets."

240.   Things you might see on a street: a car, a mother, a store, trash can, a stroller, a curb, a green light, a baby, a bus, a man

A *car* honked at a *mother* crossing the street with a *stroller*. She yelped and jumped back to the *curb* and waited for a *green light*. The light changed and she started across. In the middle of the street, her *baby* threw his rattle out of the stroller and began wailing. She couldn't leave the stroller to go back for the rattle, so she said, "Hush. We'll cross back when the light changes again, and maybe I can grab it." The baby screamed even louder. Nothing helped. Just before the light changed, a *bus* drove by and smashed the rattle.

The mother looked around, saw a *store*, and went inside. She bought another rattle, walked outside, and unwrapped it while the baby screamed. She threw the wrapper in a *trash can* and handed the baby the rattle. He stopped crying and began shaking the rattle. A *man* walking by smiled at the happy baby. "What a happy little cutie!" he remarked.

241.   Math problem: Nikola went to the grocery story with his 12 cousins and a breathable bag full of 48 ladybugs they had all collected. If he purchased eight wedges of American cheese, three backscratchers and one cactus, how many centimeters would he need to roll seven car tires, and how long would it take?

Response: 67 lasagnas

242.   Alec is very committed to his self-described luxurious locks of hair—not on top of his head but above his eyes. He has long, wild, golden eyebrows that he can brush, braid, shampoo, and condition. He really loves his unusual form of facial hair, so much so that he embraces the the nickname people have given him: Mr. Unruly Eyebrow Face. While he loves his eyebrows, they have made it hard to find someone as a partner.

Unjournaling © Taylor & Franc

Starla is proud of her powerful legs and powerful feet. She loves to bejewel them in thick-soled Dr. Martens boots. She takes giant steps that boom when she walks. She loves to imagine that she is a modern-day embodiment of an Amazon warrior. Other people don't love the startling stomping sounds she makes, especially her neighbors in the downstairs apartment. They see her as less Greek warrior goddess and more of an obnoxious person who is crushingly impossible to be around.

Well, as they say, there is someone for everyone. One day at the park, Alec sat alone on a picnic blanket enjoying the light spring breeze blowing through his eyebrows. He was suddenly electrified to hear a booming rhythm coming across the concrete pedestrian bridge. It felt like an ancient cadence calling him to something. He looked up and saw what appeared to be a powerful Amazon warrior emerging over the rise of the bridge. Her black, thick-soled boots gleamed in the May sunlight.

At the same time, Starla saw spectacular golden curls gently swaying across a glowing and adoring face. It was a mutual love at first sight!

243. Hazel Henrietta Hannah Huang is a happy human. It may not be humanly possible to imagine the heraldic heights of happiness she gleans from her H-filled name. Her sweaters each hold a hand-stitched signature H above her heart. Her favorite foods start with H: hamburgers, hoisin sauce, hoagies, ham omelets, hot pockets, Hershey kisses, honey cakes, Hostess cupcakes, hot dogs, and hummus. She spends hours watching old TV shows: *Hill Street Blues, Hart to Hart, Hawaii 5-0, Homicide,* and *He-Man* cartoons. Her hallowed hound Henry who responds to Hank is the love of her life. He humors her by playing dress up in herringbone hats in a heathered hunter green. Hazel loves haiku, hockey games, and hip hop music. She hopes to travel to Helsinki, Havana, Hong Kong, and Houston.

244. "It was such a giant mistake," said Greta, as she vomited over the edge of her roller coaster seat for the fifth time in just a few minutes. As her stomach churned, she recounted the state fair feast she had gobbled up before climbing on the festival rides. There was the giant turkey leg, the funnel cake, the corn dog, the deep fried Oreo, and the deep fried Snickers bar. Oh, and she can't forget the nachos with extra pickled jalapenos and Hot Cheetos dust. She chugged a Big Gulp sized root beer right before Armando convinced her to live a little and enjoy a ride on the Wild Chipmunk whipping roller coaster. She hoped that she had nothing left in her stomach and that she could make it back to solid ground without another barfing round, but it was August and 102 degrees outside.

245. • Would you rather walk barefoot across a really large room covered in tiny Legos OR spend the night with a cockroach in your bed?
    • Would you rather drink a gallon of rotten and chunky milk OR eat raw meat with maggots on it?
    • Would you rather listen to the loud whistle of a train all night long OR have a dental drill working on your teeth all night long?

- Would you rather pick someone else's nose and eat it OR carry a burning hot pizza pan—one that never cools off—for over an hour?
- Would you rather pierce your own nose with a thumbtack OR cuddle a feral rat like a baby for a whole day?

246. *Lamar Springfield* was an old-time crooner with classical good looks. He traveled the rodeo circuit and often sang to adoring fans in dusty old stadiums next to cornfields. While his platinum albums demonstrate that he could definitely draw large crowds in the big cities, he preferred this rural, backroad career where he could sing the music he loved and eat lots of homemade pie in local diners.

247. There is an old saying: Like a chicken with its head cut off. This is supposed to indicate wild and chaotic behavior. Headless Mike—a literal chicken with its head cut off for 18 months—defied all laws of nature and this old saying.

   Headless Mike was anything but wild and chaotic. He immediately understood the opportunity of being a headless chicken and didn't want to waste any of his uncertain time running around like the proverbial chicken with its head cut off. Instead, Headless Mike met the moment with dignity and a business mind. He knew that he could milk the public with his sensational appearance and story. He met with a financial advisor to set up a nest egg for his many descendants for after the inevitable finally happened. He got on all TV news shows and the late-night talk circuit. He established himself as an overnight Instagram influencer and charged money for people to come and witness his phenomenal appearance. He even amplified his net worth with an outrageous feathered tuxedo and a plumed hat designed for his headless body. He wore it to the annual Met Gala before collapsing to his death after a year and a half of beating the odds. His hard work paid off and his descendants will live on his fortune for generations of chickens to come.

248.   Eliza: Hey, Elias, irregardless of what you think, I am definitely the funner twin!
       Elias: Oh, Eliza, why must you destroy our beautiful language just to antagonize me?
       Eliza: We have nothing in common, but supposbly we are twins. That's what Mom says anyways.
       Elias: Sigh. Eliza, I know that you are just trying to annoy me. Unfortunately, it is working.
       Eliza: Elias! It is a ginormous bore to be so persnickety about everything!
       Elias: Persnickety? Did you just become acquainted with a thesaurus? That is a pretty big word for a self-professed butcher of language. I would rather be a persnickety bore than a tedious real-life troll.
       Eliza: Whoa! A real-life troll? I love you and you prolly know it! This is just how I show it.
       Elias: I realize in your demented sister-like ways that this is somehow endearing.
       Eliza: You truly are the bestest, my most favoritest, the most smartest, excetera, excetera!

249. Blue broke my heart. My beautiful and beloved boyfriend of a bunch of weeks just blew off our imminent betrothal before his big baseball game. I just boasted to my besties that my bae and I were bound by a blessed bliss. Our beaming bond was forever material, like the buoyant endings of my brother's bodice-busting romance books. Oh, Cupid, I beseech you. Beam your infatuating beta rays towards Blue's beating heart that once burned with love for this now besmirched ball of bleakness that is me, Bonita.

250. 1. Why would someone wear a shoe made out of glass?
   2. Why didn't Cinderella get to stay out past midnight like everyone else?
   3. Why would anyone get married after just spending a few hours at a dance together?
   4. Why were her only choices cleaning the house or getting married?
   5. Why was Cinderella's foot smaller than everyone else's?
   6. Why would the king and queen let the prince marry a penniless servant?
   7. Why do we assume the prince is charming when he is probably really spoiled?
   8. Why didn't Cinderella's father leave her some money?
   9. Why isn't it gross to put the same shoe on everybody's foot?
  10. Why wouldn't the glass slipper be smelly and sweaty after Cinderella danced in it all night?
  11. Why would we assume that Cinderella is such a dazzling date when she is probably hungry, overworked, and not used to being around people?
  12. Why didn't the stepmother and stepsisters recognize Cinderella at the ball?
  13. Why did everything magical disappear at the final stroke of midnight except the glass slippers?
  14. Why didn't the fairy godmother help Cinderella earlier by waving her magic wand to make her living conditions better?
  15. Why are stepmothers always evil characters?

About the Authors

Dawn DiPrince writes every day in her job as the Executive Director of History Colorado, the Colorado Historical Society. In this work, she heads a team that teaches, tells, and interprets the diverse stories of Colorado, and she leads community workshops where neighbors collectively write the history of where they live. She lives in Denver, Colorado, with her husband and is the proud mom of three incredible children.

Cheryl Miller Thurston taught English and writing classes, grades seven through university level, and then worked in publishing for many years. She is the author of many books for teachers, several plays and musicals, and two novels. Also a musician, she is the founder of the national organization Closet Accordion Players of America. She lives with her husband and two pampered cats in Loveland, Colorado.

DOI: 10.4324/9781003278559-4